LIFEBIRDS

LIFEBIRDS

GEORGE LEVINE

Illustrations
by Marge Levine

RUTGERS UNIVERSITY PRESS / NEW BRUNSWICK, NEW JERSEY

Library of Congress
Cataloging-in-Publication Data

Levine, George Lewis.
Lifebirds / George Levine ;
illustrations by Marge Levine.
p.   cm.
Includes index.
ISBN 0-8135-2202-1
1. Bird watching.   2. Nature.   I. Title.
QL677.8.L465   1995
598'.07234—dc20   94–41058

British Cataloging-in-Publication
information available

Text copyright © 1995 by George Levine
Illustrations copyright © 1995 by Marge Levine

All rights reserved

Published by Rutgers University Press,
New Brunswick, New Jersey

Manufactured in the United States of America

For Paul and Michael
and for the birds they have watched with me

Contents

Acknowledgments

*T*HIS IS A BOOK that is both entirely personal and utterly dependent on the generosity and affection and intellectual honesty of others. Marge Levine sustained me through it, encouraged me in what seemed a quixotic and perhaps also self-indulgent enterprise, and of course lovingly indulged me over the years in my obsessions with the birds. She has shared many of these experiences with me or has made them possible. We have, I think, learned even more of each other, after thirty-eight years of marriage and learning, from these birdy memoirs. And her wonderful powers of seeing will be visible in these pages.

Matthew and Renee Baigell were my first readers after Marge. They made me believe their praise; and their criticism, characteristically intelligent, sympathetic and precise, made me understand more about what I was doing and about what I had failed to do. They are not birders, but I forgive them because they have been my closest friends for many years.

Leslie Mitchner is always far more than an editor. Her encouragement led me to write this book in the first place, and her broad reading and critical intelligence have made her criticism of my work both entirely credible and wonderfully helpful.

The book's dedication should make it clear how much I owe to Paul and Michael, my birding companions and my good friends. Both of them read this manuscript. Paul kept me honest on many birding facts and memories. He is not responsible for the remaining bloopers. Michael became my severest and thus my most helpful critic, and if these chapters avoid the pitfalls of sentimentality, flaccidity, self-pity and self-indulgence, Michael was the reader who kept me from them. If they fall into these traps, Michael was the reader who warned me.

LIFEBIRDS

herring gull

FOR THE BIRDS

*I remember wondering why every gentlemen
did not become an ornithologist.*
—Darwin

I DON'T KNOW what kind of book this is. It came to me
with an urgency I hadn't imagined, in the middle of work
on a far different project, a book on narrative and epistemology. I have some sense now of what poets must have meant
when they claimed inspiration of a muse. My inspiration
came from winged things, creatures who have been resisting
my representation of them for more than twenty years but
who, in the end, have demanded my voice. The urgency, I
came to understand, derived not only from the birds large and
small that have been populating my otherwise wintry and academic imagination for so long; it came from the way the birds
have been inwoven into my life, professional and personal—
inwoven so completely that I had not understood their importance.

I have long vowed that I would keep birds separate from my professional life. I work with words and transform the world into texts. The importance of birds to me, I thought, is that they were precisely not texts. They resisted the strategies of literary criticism and cultural analysis by flying past our lives regardless of us, by leaving white guano on rocks, by cooing mercilessly in attic windows, by standing in the middle of the road pecking at carrion or filling the skies over garbage dumps or singing magical songs in suburban backyards or grazing our lawns or sitting beautifully in places we sometimes notice. I valued the birds because they were so distinctly not me and not grist for my literary mill. I was not going to write a paper on birds in literature. I was not going to write a paper on birds.

But in dozens of different ways that this book attempts to register without categorizing them, birds have worked their way into my life and thought and I have been forced to recognize the degree to which even their otherness is part of a distinctly human conception, bred from books and texts and language as much as from the confrontations or evasions of the field. It's hard not to anthropomorphize and I have learned to allow myself the luxury while I reserve the right to deny its validity. In my summer rental of several years we have inherited a herring gull the owners call "Gertrude." Gertrude is, I think, a male, but that doesn't matter. Gertrude has been trained to come to call regularly, usually at breakfast, and although the silliest thing in the world is feeding herring gulls—those ferociously self-sufficient parasites who are pretty good at making life miserable for smaller birds—we lay out her breakfast on the porch railing and she pecks her way down it until finished, occasionally fighting off other gulls, after which she takes off, usually not without leaving us some white spackling for the porch. I talk to Gertrude. She is getting used to me. I worry about who will feed her off-season: all sentimental self-indulgent nonsense. But if you think about it,

Gertrude is very beautiful (gulls are so common we're not used to thinking about how lovely they are), and we give each other our various kinds of human and avian pleasure.

While this book is about many other things, it is also and primarily about birds. It is written, as should be clear from the start, by somebody who is not by professional or even serious amateur understanding a very good birder. I have poor eyes, a bad sense of direction, a declining memory, a fear of the wilderness, and I suffer from a permanent resistance to "studying" birds so that I am unable to accumulate knowledge for the next field trip. And when I'm out in the field, I am slow to get my binoculars in focus and slow to locate the birds that everyone has already been watching. And finally, I make a lot of mistakes.

But I am a "birder." That's the noun birders use to describe themselves. There is a related verb, "to bird," which I use a lot, and there's a participial noun built from that verb, "birding," which is what most of the essays in this book are about. A fairly large vocabulary, which doesn't feel like jargon to birders, grows jargonishly from this birdy base. "To bird" can be used in relation to a place, so one can say, "I birded Jamaica Bay," or "I birded Central Park." When birders use the word as it should be used, that is, a "bird" is a bird, it often is not quite that. For instance, given the birder's usual penchant for listing, each "bird" is likely to have a place on some list. A "lifebird," to take this book's major example, is a bird that the birder has never seen before in his or her entire life. But then there are "yearbirds"—obviously, birds unseen until then in the course of a particular year. By analogy, there are "daybirds" and "tripbirds." In addition, there are birds defined by the places they turn up. So there are "state birds," which means not the state mascot, but a bird seen in the state. There are even "backyard birds," birds seen in the backyard. I don't know that I can in fact think of all the different ways birders use the word-root "bird." But beyond that use, there are other birding shortcuts: so a sharp-shinned hawk will become a "sharpie." A mockingbird will become a "mocker." A mourning dove, on some principle of economy, will become a "modo," and a turkey vulture will become a "tv." There are other extensions and variations that I hope will become clear as I go along.

While I am a birder absorbed happily in this often goofy language, I can't be entirely relied on when I am away from words. In writing this book, I did not try to correct my field errors, although in the end friends often corrected them for me, and I used very few reference texts. I always keep Peterson's *A Field Guide to the Birds East of the Rockies* by my side. And I always now use, both in the field and for quick reference, the National Geographic *Birds of North America*. I have for the most part stayed away from my bookshelves at home, loaded though they are with bird books, most of which I bought for the pictures. This book is not, then, a field guide to the birds. It is not even intended as a set of sketches of the various birds named at the head of each chapter. Rather, it is a gesture at an experience that matters greatly to me and, I hope, to many others: the extraordinary variety and excitement of birding, the complications and subtleties of bird identification, the implication of birding in the imagination and the world against which it is usually defined. I want to make birds attractive and interesting and I can only do that by honoring my experience of them. Although I care very much about what the birds look and sound like, this is not in any way a "scientific" text, systematically representing the birds with which it is concerned. It is about the birds, but it is primarily about the human experience of the birds. It is not meant for experts, unless they want to know how a journeyman experiences the world that to his eyes they seem to have mastered. In the end of course the book is about a lot more than birds: it is about "lifebirds."

THERE ARE only about eight hundred species that breed or pass through the continental United States and after a while an experienced birder will have seen a significant portion of that number. If, like me, you do most of your birding in the mid-Atlantic and New England states, it will become increasingly difficult for you to see a new species without traveling, say, to Nebraska, or Oregon or Texas. And since the avid birder is constantly on the lookout for species he or she has never before seen, this book passes through many states a long way from New Jersey, where I live and work. Each lifebird, I discovered, is entangled in narratives that string back into other aspects of my life. Each lifebird enriches my life a little. So writing about birds has meant writing about lots of other things and telling lots of potentially vital stories.

It shouldn't be surprising, then, although it was to me, that writing about birds has opened up a vital connection to the kinds of pleasures life, both personal and "natural," keeps offering and I tend to keep refusing. It also, surprisingly, opened aspects of myself that I had been ignoring or evading. I expect that everyone who dabbles in birding will have generally similar experiences, will value birding in ways that ramify out into their lives complexly, often secretly. It took me a while to realize what will undoubtedly be self-evident fairly quickly to any other reader: that this book about birds is also and quite centrally autobiographical. I hadn't known until well into the writing that I was using the birds for many non-birding ends, doing precisely what I had self-consciously been refusing to do. The birds became an excuse to put me and anyone who might care in contact with parts of my life that I thought I had long since forgotten and other parts of which I am not terribly proud. Using birds, however, allows for considerable evasiveness, and I regularly take advantage of that allowance as much as I can, so that the birds serve simultaneously to bring me closer to things I perhaps don't want to know about and keep me from having to confront them. But however much autobiography shoves itself forward, I don't want simply to be using the birds. This book really is about birds and not about myself. But it would also be foolish of me to ignore that it is a kind of autobiography—if a very strange kind—and that the birds have forced me into yet another risk, the risk of writing about myself.

Making birds primarily a means to an end would be a betrayal of the birds, of how I experience them, and of my sense of what birding is about. I hope and more than hope that what I am writing affirms the importance of birds as birds, of birds as part of an enormous non-human world with which we cannot afford not to engage, about which we cannot afford not to think and imagine, from which we cannot afford not to take pleasure, which means taking risks. The birds have been able to signify broad human connections for me precisely because they are not symbols or signifiers, but birds. My mind does the work, turns the yellowthroat into "el bandito," Gertrude into a pal, the hooded warbler into "the Lone Ranger." But for the most part, birds don't want me around, don't care about me—except as a threat—don't dream about me, don't show off for me, don't even ignore me because "ignoring" implies a relationship they don't have. That they live their lives without me is a significant part of what makes me love them.

Yet in the course of confronting the birds through writing this book, I have discovered a lot about me as well. As I reflected back on what I had written, for example, I became an outsider to myself and noticed with some unease that these narratives seem at times to settle into a classic literary and cultural pattern. The reflections on birds and life sometimes might be read as exercises in what Eve Sedgwick would call "male homosocial bonding." There are times when in reading this book for revision I almost heard myself calling, in Leslie Fiedler's famous title, "Come back to the raft ag'in, Huck honey." The significant relations are virtually all among men, and women too often emerge as obstacles to the birding expe-

rience. I was surprised to discover this pattern and yet that is
the shape these experiences took as I turned them into narrative, and I represent that shape without apologies. Although
birding is an avocation that women indulge as frequently as
men, the cultural and personal values through which I have
been working since I became a "birder" in 1974 are for better
or worse the values that our culture has imposed upon most
of us. While one of my small birding set is in love with an expert birder and professional editor of a birding journal, she
rarely joins us on our outings. While I have myself frequently
invited women to join me (though not when I go out with my
closest birding companions), somehow I have never developed
a significant birding relation with a woman.

As birding entered my life, I found in it a way out of my
domestic and professional complications, an escape not so
much from heterosexuality as from the emotional difficulties
that accompany it in a society so heavily misogynistic and di-
vided. I have never until reading this book thought of the
bonds I feel with my birder friends as "homosocial," but we
have each of us been aware of the way the birding trips en-
courage an intimacy and frankness difficult to achieve else-
where, and that we have often, ironically, called "male
bonding." When we use the phrase "male bonding," we always
smile and we always mean it in quotation marks, but it is hard
these days not to be self-conscious about the degree to which
our society has excluded women from its moments of warm-
est intensity. Michael, the anthropologist of our birding
group, immediately understood that the birding trips were being driven by feelings beyond birds. Too great self-consciousness about this would have seriously marred the trips, but
much of the energy that has driven me to write these narratives seems to have derived from the homosocial satisfactions
they always entail.

It surely wasn't an accident (although I would like to think
it was) that none of my long-term birding friends has been a

woman, that my wife tolerates rather than takes pleasure in my fancy, that the intense emotional connections I have felt in my birding phase have for the most part, but not exclusively, been with birds and men. My son started me birding. His mentor, Paul, became my closest birding friend. Together, and then with Michael, a friend who joined us after our birding rituals had seemed to be well set, we have lived through birding experiences that are among the richest and most satisfying of our lives and that finally open out to embrace far more than our little birding community.

I have been taken by surprise by how large "Paul" looms in this text. Paul has virtually no place in my everyday life: I see him no more than five or six times a year. Over twenty years we have rarely done anything together except "bird." Yet as I see him here, as I came to represent him, Paul is an ideal—an ideal friend, a man of absolute integrity and personal generosity, a pretty good birder, and one against whose standards I measure my birding activities and, implicitly, many other ones. I can't change this by rewriting because, as these narratives have taught me, he is as I describe him. Again, it is no accident.

I did for a brief moment think about rewriting in order to break with the all too recognizable literary tradition, but chose finally not to. The point was not to change what appeared on rereading to be a just representation of the experiences, but to live with and try to understand their possible implications. It became clear to me as I proceeded that one of the virtues of writing this kind of thing instead of books on narrative and epistemology is that the exposition of what matters to me enforces a recognition of entanglements that strictly discursive prose can evade; it implicates me in ways I cannot escape and cannot change by changing my words. I am finally more than pleased with the unapologetic affection for my fellow birders that these narratives helped reveal to me, and that has helped make possible my precarious entrance into the world of birds.

I have long been aware of how birding, so detached ostensibly from the activities of work and business and social division, is normally the activity of middle-class people—"gentlemen," as Darwin called them—with sufficient money or leisure to be able to buy the binoculars and take the time to beat around the bushes and shake the trees all over America and even the world. Meeting a genuine working-class birder is almost a more rare experience than finding a difficult lifebird. What activity seems more democratic, more open, less subject to human structures of social organization? And yet I can think of few activities that are more firmly based in middle-class values and attitudes.

There are better examples, I am sure, but I think immediately of a town called Leamington near Point Pelee in Ontario that knows very well where its resources come from. During spring migration, every motel in town announces that it welcomes birders. There is a restaurant open for pre-dawn breakfasts to serve the birders eager to catch early morning movement in the trees that plays not the routine Muzak but tapes of bird calls. As one dines on eggs or pancakes and bacon or yogurt and granola, bird song (duly identified) fills the dining room. That restaurant depends on well-heeled birders traveling from all over the world to eat its eggs and rush off to watch the birds. Michael reminds me convincingly, however, that birders are by and large slow in pushing the evidences of their economic authority and that places like Leamington and, say, Cape May are the exception. Display is unnecessary, as Michael has noted, for in its refusal of the crassness and ecological destructiveness of raw commercial power, the birding community, dressed in baggy pants and worn L. L. Bean sweaters, equipped with battered Zeiss binoculars, affirms its solid and unmistakable place in the middle class, outside the vulgarities of the grossest of popular culture.

I think I have no illusions about the way birding is implicated in the world from which it seems designed to escape. I have fewer illusions now about the degree to which, even in the activities of birding, I am personally implicated in social conditions I want to be resisting. Part of what I discovered this book is about is the implication of birding in life, in life not merely as an abstract and somehow value-laden concept, but in life as it is lived in all its tawdriness, corruption, compromises, and difficulties. I describe this world as it came to me suddenly and demandingly through my birdy muse, and I care for it no less because it is like the rest of human activity, compromised and stained. What I found myself writing was not quite what I thought it would be, but as far as my skills have been able to take me it does honor to my feelings and to the birds and people I have encountered on the way. I offer it without apologies. Nothing I have learned about birding makes me cherish it any the less. In the living, these meditations and narratives have constituted a mere fragment of a fragment of my life. But they have become for me a means to know the world and myself a little better, and they register the expansiveness of those ostensibly detached and minute birdy moments, an acknowledgment of how very much the experiences invoked here matter to me and entangle my life more richly and complexly with other lives, human and non-human.

The book may be understood as a set of meditations on various kinds of entanglement—between birds and work and family and friends and nature, whatever that is—and various ways in which we find access to life outside our own. To know birds I have had to learn a lot about all of these things and about how to see, how to reflect on what I have seen, how to assimilate what I know to what I see, how to transform what I see into knowledge. To know birds is to allow oneself new sorts of pleasures and to test out new sorts of discomforts and emotional risks. This book is a detour from my "work," a de-

tour driven by a need to pay homage to one of the most pleasurable aspects of my life, to the birds and to the world that
surrounds them, to the people who think about and love
them, to the ornithologists who classify and study them, to
the families who indulge their bird-lovers, to the friends who
develop intimacies through them, to the imaginations that
makes them matter, in their superb indifferences and astonishing adaptations and glorious colors.

prothonotary warbler

PROTHONOTARY

IT WAS A BRIGHT MOMENT in a dark year. Bird migration time in New Jersey is always a time of release—just before the heaviest green of spring, when the weather can still lean back toward winter and when, crisp, yet warm and brilliant, it feels like a new beginning. We were four in the car, having driven down from New Jersey the day before, and fresh from a predawn rising: my old birding friend, Paul, the man who introduced my son to birding and thus by indirection introduced me; an anthropologist, Michael, whom I had introduced to birding but who stayed with it now more for the anthropological than the ornithological pleasures; his adopted son, Sasha, sixteen, maniacally obsessed with birds and already, not much more than a year after he had begun, far better at locating birds and more knowledgeable about them than any of us.

We were exploring new territory for us, just northwest of Chincoteague, a dense wooded area on the Virginia coast through which we managed to maneuver almost entirely because of the detailed directions of a birders' guide to the area. The boy was complaining that we were moving too much and too fast. With windows down and his scope poised, he listened for any unfamiliar bird sound and claimed, with virtually every call, that it provided grounds for a stop. "Northern waterthrush," he shouted. Although I have a reputation for talking too much during birding tours and punning oppressively with childish witlessness, I confess to a birding enthusiasm only slightly less intense than Sasha's. I don't know why. I'm too old for that sort of thing. Unlike Sasha, I'm not willing to spend very much of my time outside of birding trips studying birds so I have never—after twenty years of enthusiasm—become a really accomplished or reliable birder.

My excitement on these trips is rather unselfconscious, and it intensifies the longer the trips last. It's bird saturation, and the relief from normal responsibilities, family connections, anxieties, is not forced, which is why it works. This world has nothing to do with mine, but it's right there just off the road. The birds don't think about me much, would—insofar as they do think about me—prefer not to have me watching them; they have other responsibilities, connections, anxieties. But while I belong to almost every conservation group that solicits money, I still risk disrupting their birdy lives just because I have come to care for them so much. And the northern waterthrush was a bird that I had always enjoyed seeing, skulking as it does in its quiet brownish ways, at the edge of lakes and ponds. Of course, I would have much preferred a Louisiana waterthrush, a bird that I am a little embarrassed to say I have never seen. The Louisiana, I know, has a white eyeline, with a touch of buff toward the bill; the northern's is buffy all the way.

These are the kinds of things I worry about on birding days. The birds aren't much more than five inches long, bill to tail (although the Louisiana is apparently perceptibly—three-quarters of an inch—larger than the northern). At Sasha's call, I tightened a bit, listened hard, tried to make the insistent, relatively high-pitched, repetitive call match my confused memory of the warbler tape I had been playing on my short trips to work every day since April 15, that is, on the edge of migration season. Since I knew that Sasha had those tapes virtually memorized, I assumed he was right about the water-thrush, but it didn't feel right. "Feeling right" is, by the way, an important aspect of birding. For people like me, at least, it's not a science.

Part of the pleasure of birding for me is getting the mind to work its way through the complexities of nature, no matter how minute a part this might be, to make its way and make some sense of it. Most of the time, I'm overwhelmed. But over the years I've been able to pick from its entanglements a sound here, a color there, a movement. When the cardinals start singing in the coldest days of late winter and early spring, I feel the presence of the spring I'm desperate for. When the grackles, with whom I will be annoyed in a few weeks, suddenly appear around my feeder in February, it's fair to say that I am genuinely happy. When I take an early morning walk around my suburban neighborhood in the summer, I am astonished to hear (only occasionally see) dozens of different if familiar bird species—well, at least two dozen: mockingbirds, catbirds, cardinals, robins, song sparrows, house finches, chickadees, titmice, flickers, downy and red-bellied woodpeckers, mourning doves, blue jays, grackles, starlings, goldfinches, house wrens, even an occasional wood thrush. I can pick them out by ear, don't have to look up, can even be reading the *Times* as I go. It feels good. At least suburban nature is not entirely alien to me. Somehow, being able to name things makes a difference.

"Northern waterthrush" didn't seem right. And then out of some resources I didn't think I had, I literally screamed, "That's a prothonotary warbler!" Michael pulled the car up sharply and we piled out. That movement was an act of confidence I could appreciate even in the rush and excitement of the moment. I had never heard a prothonotary warbler in a way that could make me or anybody else believe that I "knew its call," except perhaps on those tapes. Nobody asked if I was sure, except me. I guess I wasn't. I was simply abashed at the brashness of my call. Yet the place was right: wooded, boggy, near water. Of course, it was right for the waterthrush too, except that I *knew* it wasn't a waterthrush.

But there's an ethos of birding. Even for those who are not particularly competitive about it—and Michael, Paul, and I are self-consciously not competitive—there is an awkwardness, an embarrassment, about saying something really stupid: calling a mourning dove a kestrel, for example. Paul's closest friend is a truly expert birder, a professional editor of a major birding journal, and she once in my presence called a light fixture several hundred yards away a peregrine falcon. Things like that happen, even to the best birders, and I was not among the best. I usually find a way not to name a bird that flashes by, but only to call attention to it. I'm sure I will get it wrong and I'm pretty defensive about it. But there I was shouting "prothonotary warbler" and bringing the car to a stop and getting all my friends excited.

The bird kept calling and the more it called the more I was able to superimpose it on my memories of the warbler tape. I was even beginning to feel confident about it, but the brush was so thick and the ground was so boggy, I didn't think I would see the bird. That, for the most part, has been my relation to the prothonotary. Expert birders don't have much trouble finding prothonotaries; they know where they hang out, and every spring, the really good birders identify them. Once, on a similar trip with Paul, we spotted a bird on a dull, gray, almost drizzly day rather high on a power wire. I saw the bird. Paul saw a prothonotary. But my eyes wouldn't unfold the marks I needed for identification. It just looked gray to me. I knew Paul was right. He never claims a bird about which he is not absolutely confident, and he has taught me appropriate humility in the face of the multitudinousness and difficulties of the world of birds, and, perhaps more important yet, in the face of the deviousness of our own eyes and desires. So I didn't really *see* a prothonotary until the year I bullied Paul and Michael into flying with me out to Detroit, where we rented a car to drive to Point Pelee in Ontario, a remarkable, narrow spit of land arrowing into Lake Erie, over which virtually every migrating species coming through the midwest will travel.

For me Point Pelee was no disappointment. It provided perhaps two of the most satisfying days of my life, and it wore me out with excitement and persistence so that when I returned as happy as I have been in a very long time, I was bedridden with a violent cold and exhaustion for a couple of days. But it was more than worth it, not the least because at Point Pelee I saw my first prothonotary, off a road on the edge of the lake, sitting—almost on cue—on a power wire. He was, I think, calling; but I was so excited at the sighting that I didn't burn that call into my consciousness. It was bright, crisp, cool, and he was overwhelmingly beautiful—a deep rich gold glowing in the sun, with blue-gray wings in contrast. He sat there for a long time as if to assure me that the identification was right, characteristically, appropriately, satisfyingly indifferent to my presence. That was my prothonotary experience until the moment when I dared to identify his call, and in honor of that first sighting, I had bought a picture postcard of the bird, which sits even now on my office desk.

I had wondered a lot about that odd name. The word, "prothonotary," was one I never heard outside of the birding context. I noted the word "notary" in it, and finally checked the dictionary to see if it could help explain it. The explanation was simple. The color of the bird matched—or so the story goes—the color of the robes worn by the prothonotaries of the Catholic Church, ecclesiastics "charged with the registry of important pontifical proceedings." But there was nothing secretary-like about this bird, no metaphorical hint of writing. Birds have, for the most part, asserted their reality for me directly and healthily against language, against the worlds of textuality in which I live professionally and about which my colleagues and I theorize interminably. My love of birds may in fact stem largely from the way they confirm the reality of something outside of language and outside of my own construction. I have wanted always to preserve that world of birds from the imperialism of textuality, and until now have refused to write about birds or my experience of them—except perhaps in letters to the few friends who might care. I have wanted to insist to myself that my experience of them has nothing to do with language.

But of course, that's not true. Before I ever saw a prothonotary I knew about it through books. I studied its image in the various representations of it in *The Golden Guide*, in two different editions of Peterson's *Field Guide to the Birds*, and now most particularly in the current preferred birders' guide, The National Geographic Society's *Field Guide to the Birds of North America*, which calls it a "casual or rare vagrant across most of the continent during migration." I knew its likely habitat because of books. I read Peterson's language about it and that spoke to me rhythmically as von Humboldt's descriptions of the tropics spoke to the young Darwin: "a golden bird of wooded swamps." The language filled me with desire. I am tempted even now to pause to talk about the poetry of Peterson, except that would betray the birds. If I had read Peterson right to start with, I would have had no second thoughts about my call, for Peterson describes the bird's song so as to create it unmistakably: "zweet zweet zweet zweet zweet zweet." It's not what the bird says, but it's what we are capable of hearing. My own way of learning was harder and less precise, since I had constructed my warbler song from a tape that seemed never to say "zweet." The bird may have been even better than Peterson; yet I won't forget that call now because no prothonotary warbler will be able to say anything for me but a series of "zweets." Never again will bird song be the same.

Escape from representation and texuality may be impossible, and the bird's link to the Catholic Church will remain permanently in what we have chosen to call it, but that boggy swamp was not a book and not a representation. I find it hard to believe that the color of the Catholic prothonotary's cloak was as rich and intense as the color of the bird, just as I do not believe I have seen a scarlet in the world that can match the male scarlet tangager's. I wondered, as I began to push through the underbrush and feel the crust over the wet ground give under my feet, if I could get close enough to that zweeting bird to see it after all, to confirm my instinct for its reality (and perhaps gain a bit more respect from Sasha, who thinks I talk too much and bird too little). But I am used to being defeated by the resistances and otherness of the nature I choose to enter on these May trips. Most of the birds I hear and seek escape me unless they are being unaccountably indifferent to my presence and willing to carry on their business publicly. And as I pushed closer to the sound, the bog and the brush grew more hostile. I half gave up, and pulled back, thinking of putting on my boots, hoping the bird would get closer to the road.

Michael is always impatient with us, always goes his own way on these trips, always seems fearless about plunging into the writhing intricacies of thornpatches and underbrush, and prefers, in any case, either to watch us as anthropological specimens of the tribe, birders, or to move away from our birding intensities to see things as he wants to see them. He was impatient now, and pushed into the brush well beyond where I had ventured and then remained long and silent. Eventually, the bird still calling, Paul followed. And I went back after him. When I arrived at the spot, Michael had long since begun looking for other things as he told Paul that, yes, the prothonotary was there, just above us in that tree. Paul followed Michael's general directions and found it. I followed Paul's lead and saw only a dense green canopy.

My eyes have been deteriorating for many years. I still try to bird without glasses, hoping that I will spot the movement sufficiently with my blurry naked eye so that I might locate the bird with my binoculars. But I saw no movement. Paul, who is gentle and generous in ways that constantly touch me, tried to lead me to the bird. There, follow the second tree on the right, note where there is a large diverging branch to the left, follow it to where it intersects with another large branch, and just above that, just below the highest canopy, there's the warbler. Often Paul is successful in guiding me through such instructions. Paul is a mathematician, and his instinct for precision makes him far better in the woods than I. For my part, I am incapable of giving such instructions: I don't dare raise my binoculars from the bird long enough to see the surrounding foliage since I know I will never find it again, and because even when I do take the risk, my powers of discrimination and description are unequal to the effort to guide somebody else's eye through the tangles of a thick woodland. But Paul tried again, and again. Michael called over that Paul had unbelievable tolerance and patience. I felt both stupid and tensely frustrated. I wanted to see the bird and I clung to Paul's words as though I were in fact hanging from one of those trees.

It took far too long. The minuteness of Paul's descriptions testified to his understanding of how much was at stake for me, how much it mattered, and it testified too to his generosity. And at last it worked. This extraordinary five-and-a-half-inch golden bird of the wooded swamps was there, where he belonged, high above us in this wooded swamp, "zweet zweet zweet zweet zweet zweet," filling the entire field of my vision, so it seemed, with his gold and for me an unexpected flash of large white patches on his blue-gray tail which showed in such sharp contrast to the bright green of the thick canopy that it seemed almost black—white, black, gold—and it sat there, then fluttered across to fill my binoculars in yet another way from another branch and always "zweet zweet zweet zweet zweet zweet" assuring me that I was right, binding me to my friends in a new way, binding me to these impenetrable woods and this boggy earth, and making me feel after all how unpredictably beautiful this inextricable tangle of otherness and text and representation and fluttering, singing bird could be.

eastern kingbird

KINGBIRD

I N THE FIRST few months of my life as a birder, almost any bird seemed possible. I didn't know enough to know what I could not see, nor to expect what I could. I didn't even know—really know—that all things were not possible, that some birds would only turn up in the woods, some in swamps, some on lakes, some on oceans. I hadn't begun to learn the pleasure of limitation, the excitement of finding an aberrant bird in the wrong place at the wrong time, or conversely, the strong pleasure of finding the expected exactly where it is supposed to be. At that moment, mourning warblers, skulkers in the low brush that don't spend much time in my part of the world, were as likely as yellowthroats, an abundant breeding warbler that I still hear every day of spring and summer when I'm looking; and to distinguish the real bird I happened to be looking at I had to flip through all the pages of my field guide. Flickers were as thrilling as yellow-bellied sapsuckers. In my life list to this day an unlikely mourning warbler from my first year of birding awaits an actual sighting to turn it into a confident truth.

Now, my neighboring woods hold virtually no birding mysteries and certainly no mourning warblers; then they were a paradise of possibility, and yielded a mourning warbler to my uneducated eyes. There seemed to be enough clues in what I saw in the little warbler-like bird with yellow breast and darkish head, and so I claimed the warbler which, as my knowledge grew, unaccountably never returned to those woods or the adjoining fields. I learned to see only slowly, just as my eyes began to weaken and my prescription glasses were getting thicker. My son had abandoned me to the field alone so the field guide was all I had.

He had abandoned me to all those possibilities, I guess, because I was his father and he had introduced me to birding and could impress me with what he knew. I still believe he was a remarkably precocious birder at the age of twelve, and I have in my desk a little notebook he kept of his bird identifications at the time (a notebook, it should be clear, he has never missed). I was then skeptical of birding enthusiasms, partly because my brother had been a really excellent birder when I was a very little boy with no interest in birding at all. I knew only that he would go out in zero weather, return ten hours later with horror stories of friends who were frostbitten and grand claims for having seen a remarkable variety of birds with absurd names. From those days until my son, David, took up birding, I never seriously looked at a bird, although I did sometimes boast that my brother was an excellent ornithologist who went to the University of Wisconsin and studied with Aldo Leopold.

But David was my son, not my brother, and his enthusiasm pleased and enticed me. I would occasionally act as chauffeur to him and his friends and drive them through bird sanctuaries. Not infrequently, they would shout the name of some bird that excited everyone in the car but me, who didn't know that such a bird existed, and I would slam on the brakes and they would leap out as I sat looking on amused and distant. (I have since learned that my ignorance kept me from seeing a Lapland longspur in full breeding plumage on one of those trips, and now I can measure that stupid loss in the likelihood that I will never, in all my life, see one.) These trips had their effect, however, and David's enthusiasm imperceptibly changed my way of thinking and feeling about birds, or, to put it perhaps more honestly, made me for the first time think and feel about birds at all.

So when we returned from my sabbatical year in England we went out together, down to the local river, a habitat he thought would be comparable to the habitats he knew as he learned birding with my friend Paul, the mathematician, who was not his father. There wasn't much down by the Raritan River that we could see or he could show me. (Now, years after David has left, I see herons and egrets there and cormorants, too.) I do remember working out with David's scrupulous assistance that one of the few shorebirds to be seen was a yellowlegs, although we had no idea whether it was a greater yellowlegs, or a lesser yellowlegs. At least it had yellowy legs.

David probably saw that I was getting into it, threatening to become the enthusiast I did become after he abandoned me, perhaps capable of becoming better at it than he (I still wonder whether here, as in other things, he overestimated me). In any case, when I would invite him for a bird walk or to plan a birding trip, even with Paul, he increasingly found ways to lose his interest. I don't think that from those days when he turned thirteen, he has ever gone birding on his own initiative again.

That was a loss, and to both of us. But the loss had its gains. I will always think of birding as my son's gift to me, a gift that remains in many ways inexplicably significant and health-giving and that has helped, after long separation and in paradoxical and circular ways, to move us back toward each other again. Not least of the compensation for that early loss has been the extraordinary sense of possibility and revelation I first felt when I went out into the field myself and, with no oedipal tensions in the air, struggled to make some sense of the winged creatures that to my astonishment had apparently always inhabited my neighborhood without my seeing them. When I first caught a goldfinch in my binoculars, I thought it was huge and gorgeous. It was more astonishing to discover that it was small and gorgeous and that I didn't need to walk into the woods to find it.

I learned that I had not been seeing and came to feel that there was everything to see. To bird well I simply had to see the world around me better, more precisely, more carefully. I'm sure that David himself had no sense that my birding was significantly connected to him; my guess is that in a short time he came to feel that my relation to birds was rather like my relation to work, another way in which I managed not to see him and to be obsessive. Yet it was a gift, if perhaps a little too late to make the kind of difference we both might have wished. For a while I was sorry that I had to go out birding alone. Since there was no adequate field guide to the family, I took the field guide to the birds.

I have no other regrets about birding except that I haven't been able to see more and better. And I mark the beginning of my life as a birder some time after David lost interest. It was early July of my forty-third year. That's rather a late date to turn birder. My family had gone off on holiday but I had a lot of work to do before I could catch up with them, and I found myself alone one Sunday morning with my recently purchased binoculars, no son to make me feel guilty and inadequate, no family responsibilities, and no knowledge. Uncharacteristi-cally, I declared myself free to do what I pleased, and I pleased to take my binoculars down to a park by the side of the river where there were stretches of relatively untouched woods. Of course, I didn't know what I was looking for, and I was a little dubious that a crowded park, however green, was likely to produce much wildlife. But I strolled, binoculars at the ready, through a field some distance from where families were beginning to set up their picnics.

A bird darted away from the picnic areas into a solitary, heavily leaved tree on the margin of the field and I knew about it only that it was a bird I didn't know. I could see it plainly enough but couldn't name it. In what I was to learn was a characteristic reaction, my stomach began to tighten and my heart to quicken out of frustration at not knowing what I was seeing and excitement at the possibility of a discovery. There was a curious pleasure in that sort of tension—the focus was entirely on a bird and my own capacity to encounter it intelligently. I knew there was every chance I would never find out what it was. Most of the time, even as I have become a more experienced birder, I do not find out: part of what I have experienced as important remains permanently inexplicable. (Paul reassures me with one of his sage birding aphorisms: "Not every bird was meant to be identified.") But as I began birding by myself, I had the sense that if I really got good at it, every bird would be knowable. And this bird, sitting quite clearly before me, *had* to be known. I could know it. But then, how to see it so that it would identify itself?

It wasn't, at least, a robin, although it was about robin size. That kind of instinctive comparative notation of size turned out to be very smart. Accomplished birders taught me later that size comparison is an important strategy for seeing. David and I would have had no trouble with the yellowlegs if we had seen it together with its "lesser" or "greater" cousin. Birds' sizes are deeply deceptive unless you can see *your* bird in relation to some other whose size you know. This robin-sized bird was dark and moved abruptly when it flew, although I'm not sure that I was able to register that quality of its movements at the time. Happily, as I walked warily closer to the tree and actually got quite a good look at it sitting exposed on a branch, against a background of green, it remained there, practically begging me to identify it so that it could get on with its business.

But I wasn't having any luck. I could say to myself, virtually aloud, to impress myself with the facts, that it was gray-black, that it had a longish tail, and that its head didn't seem quite round though it certainly had no crest. I was getting what seemed to me at the time an unusually good look at it, but I somehow wasn't seeing it. The field guide offered me a prime suspect—an eastern kingbird—except that Peterson's kingbird had a red patch on its head, while my bird, whose head from rear and front was at different moments fully visible to me, surely didn't have such a patch. I hated to keep looking down at the book because I expected that when I looked up the bird would be gone. In later years, as I have grown more experienced, I have tried to find a way to defer the reference work for the immediacy of the bird in the field, but my anxiety about identification and the surprising cooperativeness of this bird kept me thumbing through Peterson's pages and looking up intermittently to try to make a match. This was one of those birds, which I later found to be rare in my experience, that seemed content to wait while I rummaged in the field guide. As it sat there, confident and unafraid, I checked out all the gray-black birds, from loons and cormorants to mockingbirds, that might match what I was seeing so clearly and so closely through my binoculars. If this one had a red patch, I would have seen it.

Moving behind the bird, I saw what seemed pure gray-black from head to tail. I paged back to that kingbird, getting desperate now, when I noticed in Peterson a little arrow pointing to a white band at the end of the kingbird's tail. It was as though the arrow had leaped from the page because when I looked up my pure gray-black bird had mysteriously acquired a white tailband. It was hard for me to believe that it had been there all the time and that I hadn't seen it. There, however, it was, and that, as Peterson would say, was "diagnostic." Those wonderful little arrows in Peterson are marks of certainty, and the certainty of the text had become for me at that moment a glorious certainty of nature. It was a kingbird! I had worked it out for myself, and with Peterson's sanction I had no doubt.

Such moments come upon me even now, twenty years into birding, and with surprising frequency. This morning I unexpectedly discovered a little blue-gray bird in the trees behind my summer rental, and I wasn't ready for it. I caught a flash of white outer tail feathers and regularity of color, even as the bird fluttered relentlessly from branch to branch, leaf to leaf, and exhausted me with its energy and the demands on my aging reflexes. What could that bird be, acting like a peculiarly nervous warbler but too regularly blue-gray for any of them, and too small for a junco, which also has white outer tail feathers and is gray? It took a while. It was something obvious that my mind was too slow to remember. In the end, I surrendered just a little bit more of my confidence in myself as birder and returned to the field guide. Suddenly I remembered the gnatcatcher, a bird I more normally see during migration season. A little embarrassed and pleased that none of my birding friends were around, I checked Peterson, just to be sure. And there was that wonderful arrow, pointing at the white outer edges of the cocked tail of the blue-gray gnatcatcher. Diagnostic. That was my bird!

It's hard to explain or justify the excitement and satisfaction I feel when I have, however belatedly, worked it through, found it out, named the bird. The birds surely don't care; they're not affected by it, and they have their own lives to live and worry through; yet from the moment I found I could name them on my own, they entirely changed for me. The flash of recognition and confidence is so rare in the rest of my life, in scholarship, friendship, or love, that it comes to me, in those few illuminated moments when it does come, out there among the birds, as a kind of blessing. For an instant I feel a little less alien and separate. I take that gift from my son, whose relation to my developing birding passion I could not and cannot guess, but who left me to the birds on my own.

For both of us, birding may have been a means of growing up, for me belatedly. David's shift away from birds into worlds that I could not enter left him independent and shaky, but finding his way. Alone with the kingbird, I for the first time confronted the natural world with no assistance, with only my own perceptions, with no resources but those I had chosen. David's better eyes surely would have caught the white tail-band, and he might have taught me something new. With my weakening eyes, I taught myself. It's harder that way, of course, but there may not be a better way.

Now when I get good looks at a kingbird (and I almost always do since their behavior on that first day is quite typical for them), I feel a particular surge of affection and pleasure. It was the first bird that I really saw, or saw as a birder should. I have never, after all, seen the red patch, which, Peterson notes, is "rarely seen" (so why draw it on the bird in the field guide?—because it is there whether we see it or not, I guess). The guides, moreover, invariably draw kingbirds' heads as rounder than my experience of them. But I have seen kingbirds, often noisy (or, as Peterson says, "bickering"), always aggressive except when they are sitting, frequently still on a branch or wire, asking to be identified. And I see them with confidence, picked out from the endless possibilities of bird-life with which my birding imagination began.

snowy owl

SNOWY

I DON'T GET a lot of time to go out birding. My expeditions—which can last from two hours to three days—are almost invariably determined by other responsibilities, and I had strong reasons for bringing birding into my life in that marginal way. There are lots of stories, for instance, of birding divorces: one partner wants all vacations and much other time devoted to the birds; another is simply not interested. Tensions develop. Real conflicts of feeling, real failures of connection are exposed. As soon as I became aware that birding could be serious in this way, I stepped back from my enthusiasms. Even on my first trip to the Yucatan, a paradise of birds, I only allowed myself the time before breakfast to take my binoculars and see what might be seen. So my birding year is shaped by work and family, and only in the spring do I push hard for extended time alone, or with my birder friends, out in the field. As a result, there are strange gaps—strange at least to other birders—in my knowledge and experience.

The satisfaction I derive from birds not all that difficult to find suggests that my birding life is pretty severely circumscribed, and one of the curiously satisfying consequences of that circumscription is that there is always some bird, not entirely obscure or difficult, that I haven't yet seen and that I am dying to see. This puts an extra edge on the field trips. It took me almost fifteen years to see my first peregrine falcon, and that great event only happened after the restoration project that has brought peregrines back to nests even in New York City had proved its effectiveness. Now, I see peregrines every year, but they still have about them not only their intrinsic power and grace but that aura of difficulty that has more to do with me than with the bird. That prothonotary warbler of the wooded swamp was another bird I waited a long time to see—more, in fact, than fifteen years. And perhaps my longest holdout, which chose at last to reveal itself if in a very undramatic way, was the snowy owl—by reputation a wondrously ghostlike arctic raptor, starkly white with dark flecks, thoroughly out of place, one would have thought, in the commonplace urbanities and human excesses of New Jersey, New York, and environs.

The special bird, the exotic bird, is crucial to the birders' life, but for a birder like me, the failure to find it helps sustain the excitement of birding itself. Most of my greatest pleasures in birding have not really come from the rarities. I rarely give chase to the birds announced on the New Jersey rare bird alerts, but once when a lark-bunting was spotted within a half mile of my house and I chased it down with my friend Michael, the whole experience seemed banal, hardly more than an occasion to mark a bird down in my life list of birds. The bunting was indistinguishably grazing with a flock of house sparrows near a stable. Some enthusiasts spotted it for us, pointed it out, and left. Michael thought the quarter mile trip to the park wasn't worth it for so undistinguished a bird. I was moderately glad that I had troubled. That is to say that not all birding experiences are thrilling, and there aren't many rarities I would trade for my second sighting of the prothonotary. Still, I was eager to find the snowy owl, a bird that is seen regularly but not abundantly in the winter, at places like Jones Beach or Liberty State Park in New Jersey.

Since, however, I do not allow myself unanticipated pursuits of newly announced rarities, or long detours to the appropriate habitats of the birds I want to see, I measure out my birding life in small doses in circumscribed areas by the cycle of the seasons. The birding year climaxes in the spring migration when it is difficult for me not to be thinking about what's going on in the woods and fields only minutes from my office, my house, my classrooms. From about the 20th of April through the 20th of May, I struggle quietly to keep my calendar clear, to avoid unexpected meetings, even visits from old friends. I do what I have to do, which in late April and early May is a lot, especially because it is the time when graduate students invariably complete their long delayed examinations or papers, and the work of the academic year has to be rounded off, reported upon, summarized, evaluated. I recall an early morning orals exam that followed three post-dawn hours in the woods, in which I examined the candidate and picked wood ticks from my neck at the same time. Whatever my obligations, I try to get to the woods every day of that season, but if I manage to get out five or six times early on weekday mornings and to get a couple of weekend days and the big trip, usually with Paul and Michael, I have to be satisfied.

The end of spring migration usually means a relapse into very sporadic birding. Although the summer gives me much more time to look at birds, the birds won't cooperate. They are through singing loudly and amorously, with their own family responsibilities taking over. When they breed, birds don't have to sing their mating songs and they don't move around as much since their territorial spaces have all been finally defended. There is still bird song, but much less of it, and you have to be alert to catch just a fragment of a song that a month before was full-throated and complete. The migrants, of course, are gone.

Autumn brings another migration, but it comes at an extremely demanding time when there is no possibility of deferring responsibilities. University life starts up seriously when the passerines are coming back my way and the hawks are soaring south over the ridges of the Appalachians. During the fall, I usually don't find more than an odd weekend and at least one fairly formal trip to a place like Hawk Mountain, but the cultural and business rituals of September and October have to take precedence and they pull me into the winter with a persistent sense of having missed something.

During the hard days of winter, when my birding is pretty much confined to my backyard feeder, I keep a list in a drawer in the kitchen. Chickadees, titmice, cardinals, blue jays, goldfinches (in their drab olive garb), house finches and more house finches, house sparrows, mourning doves—these perfectly respectable birds constitute my birding life. When the red-breasted nuthatch appears, it's an occasion. Some recent years I have had Carolina wrens pick at the suet. And when the odd stranger turns up, for instance, the pine siskin—which is common in some areas but rare in my backyard—I take that pleasure with me through the day. This year, for only the second time in my life, redpolls appeared at my feeder (though only twice, while they were reported by the thousands throughout New York and New Jersey). This kind of birding is not insignificant, but somehow, a nuthatch in the woods is more exciting and liberating than a nuthatch seen from my kitchen window. And I get a kind of cage fever that can be cured only by serious, non-domestic birding.

Paul and I, aware of the inevitability of that fever, self-consciously and abstractly pick long in advance a deep winter weekend when we will make our Montauk trip. Out at the edge of Long Island, about as far into the Atlantic as you can get in my part of the world, Montauk is a place where the sea ducks flock at dawn. So we fight off other appointments, other responsibilities, and on a Friday in early January we drive out to the east, away from our bird feeders and our universities and our social, personal commitments. I suppose you could call it "male bonding" but I reject any negative implications that current jargon might imply, and it would be impossible without the birds. It's astonishing how long one can go on without talking of anything else. In the long run, of course, lots of other things do come up—how our children are doing, children who used to know each other pretty well, how our work is going, how we are thinking—and often we find ourselves in fascinating, pretty abstract intellectual discourse about issues that do somehow manage to bridge the gap between the scientist and the humanist, or so it seems as we drive to our next birding stop. For both of us, two people who now *only* see each other on these birding excursions, these trips are occasions for intimate and entirely unconstrained relaxation into a world we love but to which our access is closed most of our daily lives. It helps that we find we really like and trust each other.

Setting the date so long in advance is usually a problem. While it makes it possible for us to ensure that we will have the time, it also makes it impossible for us to be flexible in relation to the weather. Early January in New York and New Jersey can be brutal. We have often gone out into temperatures close to zero Fahrenheit and tramped through crusted snow and sand drifts—where snowy owls ought to be if they are going to be anywhere in our neighborhoods—doing our best to convince ourselves that we were having pleasure while keeping as tightly behind our protective gear as we could. Standing on the jetty at Jones Beach looking for purple sandpipers, with the temperature around ten degrees and the ocean wind ripping through five or six layers of clothing, is something it is usually better to talk about than to experience. Except that neither of us would forgo that experience.

Since I like my comforts and am not, outside of birding, a genuine outdoorsman, I find it a little difficult to explain the pleasure of those often painful excursions. But when, out on the jetty, the purple sandpipers appear, darting among the rocks, just out of reach of the most violent surf, sometimes almost blending into the rocks themselves, and purple in a distinctly unroyal and undramatic way, warmth wins out after all. Neither Paul nor I doubts that this is the right place to be, and the right time. Sometimes, too, there is a rather extravagant bonus at that jetty. Off its furthest point, bobbing absurdly high and erratically in the very rough water, a small duck that is worth the winter occasionally turns up. The harlequin, whose name suggests something of its variegated markings and which may be the most beautiful (and among the smallest) of the sea ducks, always gets announced on the rare bird alert when it appears. It's not terribly rare, but you never see the harlequin in numbers (at least I never do), and I have spent several winters without seeing it. Even if it were common, it would be worth announcing, for it's the duck that gives me the most pleasure, except perhaps for the wood duck, a very different, much more common, and yet more elaborately ornate creature.

Given the rarity of our excursions, the fact that not all birding trips turn up a lot of birds or any thrillingly beautiful or difficult ones seems particularly sad. Yet in their curious, often bird-scarce ways, the trips have always been successful. When we go out, we are up against a world that rarely matters much to us in our workaday lives. When we're looking for birds, we are dependent on the kindness of nature, and that's not a good position to be in. Nature cares no more for us than the birds do, and the terms of our workaday lives don't apply on these trips; the demands we make for ourselves change also. We don't really expect much from nature: the bitter cold, the rains and snows, the difficult terrain, the perverse silence of the birds are part of the pleasure. The birds become a superb excuse to see the ocean in the dead of winter, to watch the dawn over a marsh, to settle into twilight in the chill of the open fields in the spring. We never sightsee as we go, but we often catch ourselves saying something about the clarity of the light, the reflections in the still water, the turbulence of the sea.

Several years ago, after an evening in a chilly Montauk motel of a kind I probably wouldn't be willing to stay in while on holiday, and one of the few that remains open at that time of year, Paul and I woke well before dawn as usual. We wanted to get a little breakfast at a fisherman's cafe to sustain us through the chill of our wait at Montauk Point, timed to allow us to catch the first astonishing movements of vast flocks of scoters and eiders as the light comes up in the east and the birds move around the point from south to north. We knew we would see the three scoters—black, white-winged, surf, distinguishable at great distances because of a few "diagnostic" marks—and at least the common eider, and probably a couple of kinds of loons, and horned grebes, and maybe if we were quick and sharp enough an alcid or two. It would be almost like being at sea. We had done this more than a dozen times before and had never been disappointed and had never—to our surprise—suffered frostbite.

By the time we got to the parking lot at the point it was snowing very heavily and there was still no hint of dawn. The light from the lighthouse spun through a curtain of flakes. We had never given up on these expeditions before, however, and we wouldn't give up now, so we walked down softly through the deepening snow to the deck just above the beach. It did seem hopeless. There was no sound but the muffled surf and the ominous hiss of the heavy snow thickening around us. Optical equipment would be useless in these conditions. Visibility was virtually nil. We couldn't even see the ocean.

And then we heard a bird calling, a curious, rich "taweedle" kind of sound, coming not from the ocean but from the parking lot we had just left. It took us a moment to realize what we were hearing. It was no duck but a passerine, and one that I had always associated with the spring, especially with migration time. We listened carefully again, thinking it some illusion. Chilled, whitened in the now incipient dawn, we heard it again. Peterson describes the sound as "tea-kettle, tea-kettle, tea-kettle." I had never heard it in the snow. But it was unmistakably a Carolina wren, a bird whose name evokes a very different climate and whose voice always seems to have spring in it. Disappointed in the white darkness, we were suddenly cheered and smiling at this ridiculous aberration, or so it seemed to us. It turns out that Carolina wrens have been residing through the winters here in the Northeast in increasing numbers, and Michael, who was not with us this snowy day, had heard it in that parking lot on warmer winter days in previous years; but it was amazing to me that it persisted here under these deep wintry conditions. It was warm and comic relief, substituting for our invisible and inaudible sea ducks. The snow had intensified so much that we knew it was mere obsession to continue to try for the ducks, so we headed back for the parking lot, where the wren had increased the regularity and determination of its song. It was an occasion for laughter and admiration, that five-and-three-quarter-inch voice teakettling into the snow, into the darkness illuminated by flashes of the lighthouse beam whitening the dense air, calling the spring. A wren in a blizzard was, after all, worth the trip.

That wren, which we have heard again on other bitter mornings at the point, was, snowy and invisible, as satisfying as my first sighting of the snowy owl, on a relatively mild winter day in strong sunshine. We had heard of snowy sightings out near Shinnecock Bay, in southern Long Island, a frequent stopoff for Paul and me on our way to Montauk. There's a long auto causeway that curves over the bay, and as we traversed it we really had our minds set on snowys. Paul, who has seen many in his richer, longer, and more sophisticated birding life, was eager to show me one at last. He had tried for years, but while he would find snowys on other trips, with his ornithologist friends, he could never, even in the same places, find one for me. So we turned right off the overpass, pulled into a siding just back from the bay, and edged up to the water.

We looked out across at mudflats, little odd-shaped islands on which birds often sat, along with debris of various kinds. We were on the lookout for anything white, and I recalled my most recent near miss of a snowy when, in the company of a professional birder, we thought we had one. Across the Raritan, not far from a dump which used to produce both unpleasant odors and extraordinary numbers and varieties of birds, we could see a white object huddled among some low browned-out grasses. Wade, the ornithologist, wavered for a bit and then assured me that it was a snowy. I looked intensely. I believed him. But I couldn't quite make out the shape. The distance was too great, and my eyes insufficiently strong.

It was clear by the way Wade kept looking back to it that he wasn't absolutely certain. There was no movement. We left the area and returned. The "bird" was still there. My eyes still wouldn't yield the secret, but I was just about ready to admit that I had, at last, seen a snowy. That was when Wade backed down. No, he conceded, it was just a paper bag.

Paul and I saw a paper bag out on the mud flat. It was rather an owly bag, but neither of us could make out enough to think it anything but a bag. We knew how often desire had transformed inanimate objects into rare birds, and we weren't going to make my first snowy a potential paper bag. So we left the area, moved farther down the bay, and set up our scopes again. From another angle, the bag was still there. And then another birder, with a wonderful Kowa scope drove up, set up, and casually asked, "Did you see the snowy?"

The Kowa yielded the snowy truth. Through it I could see the head pretty clearly, even saw it twist, although the bird remained, for the most part, motionless. It was a lifebird, and I performed an absurd ritual to which Paul introduced me, the "lifebird dance," which means clumsy, celebratory, spasmodic movements, betokening irrational joy—which, indeed, I felt. But that snowy, sitting in the mud, was not my imagination of the snowy, not the snowy I have seen featured in bird magazines, swooping whitely against the white snow of the tundra, majestic, mysterious, powerful. It was a cute, dumpy, remote blob of whiteness in the disenchanting brightness of the winter sun, across the waters of Shinnecock Bay. Paul and I agree that we don't claim a new bird unless we have absolutely decisive evidence and unless the sighting is a satisfying one. Well, this bird, potentially regal, but utterly still, self-evidently snowy but with no indication of mystery or power, was just satisfying enough to make it absurd not to claim seeing it. But it didn't have about it the strength of that snowy Carolina wren, hidden in the parking lot at the point, or the wondrous color of the prothonotary flashing among the backlit green of the wooded swamp, or even the revelatory white band of my first kingbird.

But there is pleasure even in bathos. It was a lot more exciting than the lark bunting and I'm assuming that it will not be my last snowy. I now have to wait for that second sighting, which I am doing with an almost lifebird enthusiasm. I am not, of course, sanguine about the possibility of seeing the snowy as I dream about it—regal, low over the tundra, mysteriously powerful and dominant in the landscape. Yet this immobile snowy had its own dignity and had earned (with the help of a Kowa scope) the lifebird dance I performed for it.

sandhill crane

CRANES

IT WAS A DREARY night in November as I thought back on an already difficult autumn and looked ahead to an even bleaker winter. At my desk in the evening, work was on my mind only as a burden. Age was coinciding with the bleakness of November. My wife's mother had recently suffered an attack so severe that when we reached her house after the emergency call triggered by the device she carried with her for just such a moment, we were met by a frightening bellow that seemed to be coming through an amplifier: it was her breathing, like some demonic engine, not rasping but straining, roaring, grinding with an energy so exhausting it seemed that it could only mean death. The emergency squad worked on her with impressive efficiency and concern, but the roar continued into the hallway, into the street, and then into the ambulance outside.

For me, there was something displaced and uncanny about the whole event. Such scenes are television commonplace, and here I was, husband and son-in-law, yet a spectator again whom everyone was trying not to notice—or not so much trying but simply not noticing. My job seemed to be to stay out of the way. I contemplated help but I saw by the way Marge was moving that I was helpless to succor her, especially since she was so good at responding to crises. I was potentially useful only as driver, but Marge left the house in the ambulance. The whole scene played out before what I was surprised to discover was my detached perception of it, almost as though it were a soap opera, except that spectatorship wasn't legitimate here. I found myself knowing I should be worrying but unable to focus: How is Marge feeling? How will she handle her mother's passing? What will it do to our Christmas holiday plans? Are we going to get any sleep tonight? Should I be working at the university tomorrow? How will I feel when her mother, who, after all, I have known for close to forty years, dies? What will happen to the cat?

None of my reflections that night or on this night in November made me feel particularly good about myself. Mine was not a respectable depression. This darkening autumn was bringing with it all sorts of night thoughts—questions about my relations with the people about whom I care most, questions about the meaninglessness of my work, into which I had enthusiastically thrown most of my adult life and out of which I had earned some respect and a good salary, questions about the decay of my body and the maddeningly chronic most trivial symptoms of decline—peeing too much, seeing less clearly, bulging around the waist, growing hair in the ears and on the nose, graying and balding, wincing from pressure on the knees so that I had to give up running for the Nordic Track. Professionally, I knew that I had peaked. Momentum continued to win me respect, but no major university other than my own was likely to offer me a job if it could find someone twenty years younger and at least as smart. I guessed I was at my last stop.

It was a good stop, to be sure. I wasn't eager to leave, only for signs of my own vitality. As I looked over my desk, covered with class notes, memos relating to my administrative position in the university, books unread, partly read, overread, notes for essays and a book that nobody would care about, crazy pens that I collect because they are crazy, several tops that I spin when I am thinking hard, I noticed my little pile of bird-related magazines in the overrun on the floor. I picked off the top a recent number of a journal published by the Nature Conservancy and thumbed through looking for something enlivening, the usual gorgeous picture of some recovered wilderness or an unusual animal. But among the listings in the back—the pictures weren't that good this dreary evening—I noticed a six- or seven-line announcement of a crane watch. In mid-March the Conservancy was conducting a little tour to watch sandhill cranes in Grand Island, Nebraska.

And I remembered that on my trip to Utah the preceding year, where I went to teach in part so that I could check the birds on the Great Salt Lake, we had stopped at a motel in Grand Island decorated everywhere with pictures of cranes. I spoke to the clerk at the desk about them and she assured me that if I were in Grand Island in March, I would in fact see thousands upon thousands of cranes, just as the pictures implied. Well, here was my chance. It didn't even seem odd to me that as I thought through the most serious questions of my life and of my wife's, I found what felt like a potentially redeeming imagination of vitality and abundant life in Grand Island, Nebraska. Not a lot of my friends would understand that. Happily, if only because she had lived with me for thirty-five years, Marge would.

Without consulting anyone, I booked for the trip and felt good about it. I was doing something that I had never done— doing something. I had seen sandhill cranes only once before, on a trip to Texas where I lectured for two days and then gave myself the luxurious pleasure of flying to Brownsville and driving from there along the border up the Gulf to Aransas. Aransas was well known for the whooping cranes, so the sandhills came to me then as a delightful bonus. But my focus was on the whoopers, who were nearly extinct, and who began arriving in their last remaining cluster, fresh from their breeding season in Canada, in late October, when I got there too. In the spring they would return to Canada by way of Grand Island. I saw only a handful of cranes, perhaps a dozen sandhills and three whoopers, but "only" does not capture the experience: few as they were, both species of crane were lifebirds for me. From then up to that dreary November night, I had never seen them again, even though sandhills are not rare. What would it be like, I was wondering, to see cranes not by the handful but by the thousands?

I booked for two, thinking that I could persuade Marge or my birding friends to join me. Marge agreed to go—not being a particular fan either of Nebraska or of the cranes, although she preferred the latter—if I couldn't get somebody else. So I shipped a lot of money off to the Nebraska Conservancy and gave myself the vision of a moment when I would be out of the grim November darkness of New Jersey, my work, my sense of decline, and the prospect of the death of Marge's mother. What better bird than a crane for such release?

The winter turned out to be worse than the autumn, all difficulties compounded by the brutalities of nature that I usually attend to only when I am out birding and that I receive in another way under those conditions. The cold and the snow were relentless. Movement anywhere was extremely difficult and uncomfortable. True, the bitterness of the winter probably accounted for the influx of redpolls, some few of which appeared at my feeder and brightened things temporarily, and for a similar explosion of siskins. But I wasn't happy, and I kept the imagination of dancing cranes and the remoteness of central Nebraska before me.

Cranes became my subject of choice in the months that followed. Friends who know I love birds often tell me that they have seen a crane somewhere nearby—on the river, or on the edge of the bay as they pass by. I'm pleased that they tell me, and I often regard anybody who makes bird comments to me or asks bird questions as a possible convert. If there are few conversions, it may be because I am often rather indelicate in letting them know that they are, of course, seeing great blue herons. "There are no cranes around here. You must mean a heron. Was it blue-gray with some white on its face?" It was, anyway, very tall. For anyone who would listen, I would explain the difference: the sandhill is probably just an inch or two smaller than the great blue, which is one of the biggest American birds. As the National Geographic guide describes it, the crane differs from the heron in that it has a "bustle." If it doesn't have a bustle, it isn't a crane. (Michael perversely rejects the metaphor: but check out the drooping-feather rears of standing cranes, and there can't be any question.) In addition, the crane's bill is shorter, less "daggerlike," and it prefers prairies to tidal flats, which is why I was going to Nebraska to see it. Bird pedantry aside, all winter long cranes as more or less forced subject were comic relief, an occasion for human connection. I enjoyed the ironies at my expense, and the absurdity of looking forward to March in Nebraska while in New Jersey in December. I used the laughter as an excuse to talk about birds and if I became the buffoon in the story, that was okay. Crane conversation gave some energy to the winter, or at least to me.

We made it slowly through the year, with some reprieves before March. In January, Marge's mother was somehow managing again, though dangerously vulnerable to further attacks, and we took the chance of leaving her to visit our son in New Mexico for a few days. Out there, to our enormous relief, the sun was actually shining and the temperature was relatively comfortable, two conditions we hadn't experienced for a long while. And David was obviously trying, in ways that were never easy for him, to make us comfortable. He had thought enough about what the visit might mean to me to arrange for a stop at some famous bird sanctuaries. I was very pleased, and we found several hundred sandhill cranes at both Bitter Lake and Bosque del Apache, which Marge seemed to enjoy as well, given the stunning landscapes juxtaposing the aridity of the Southwest with abundance of water; at Bosque we saw four whooping cranes as well.

The whoopers were probably raised by sandhills in a program designed to save them from extinction. Their whiteness, at whatever distance, made them easy to spot and ostensibly totally distinct from their grayish and slightly smaller cousins. But, having been hatched by sandhills, the whoopers clearly thought they were sandhills. Their love lives would be determined by sandhill standards of beauty, and the program to save them was on the rocks because, few enough to start with, they were very unlikely to breed successfully with other whoopers. Still, even as I sensed failure, I reveled in the whooping cranes, as well as in the, for me, surprising, strange, high-pitched, slightly querulous gobbling call the sandhills made, announcing their presence long before we could see them.

The birds accompanied a lot of good, if occasionally strained, feeling. David has worked hard in recent years to overcome the tensions that forced his abandonment of birding and his resistance to me in adolescence. He has usually been the mature one in an attempt to work out some relationship that would honor all of those extraordinarily mixed feelings he has about me, not the least of which, I am sure, is love. The birds were a tacit gesture of reconciliation, a continuation of our interrupted little trip down to the Raritan. After this, I thought perhaps I didn't need Grand Island as restorative— until the return to New Jersey, winter, and illness disabused me of that fantasy.

Still, I wondered, what's the point of a crane trip if I have already seen the birds, and in some numbers? And I have even seen whoopers, who are not likely to be in Grand Island in March. Sandhills and whoopers in March would add not at all to my year bird list, and in all likelihood, many of the cranes I was seeing in New Mexico would be waiting for me in Grand Island.

But it isn't as though the checkmarks on the bird list are enough. Those marks are notations of a complicated experience worth having a lot more than once—it's not the case, to paraphrase some president or other, that if you have seen one crane you have seen them all. So it wasn't finally a difficult question. I wanted that multiple crane experience, and when I discovered that in Grand Island we were talking not about a few or several hundred but about as many as half a million cranes, I had no doubts. As Michael and Sasha and Paul all insist, ticking off species is not what birding is about. Half a million of anything was likely to produce an experience of what was for me an unimagined order, and half a million cranes sounded a lot like paradise. When I returned from New Mexico, and winter with all its accompanying dissatisfactions returned too, Grand Island seemed just as attractive as it had before. It cut in at right angles to the dead level of the chilly year, and now, at least, I had an intimation of what I might be encountering, how the cranes sound, what they might look like when crowded together. In addition, as I pointed out to Marge and anyone else who would listen, the Nature Conservancy brochure tantalizingly assured us that on the last morning, at dawn, we would be out hearing "the booming of the prairie chickens." Since I had never seen, no less heard, a prairie chicken, that was more than comic attraction.

Unfortunately, Paul was going to Mexico. He wanted to try the cranes, but he had arranged for the Mexican trip with his editor friend before I had even thought of Grand Island. I confessed that if I had had a choice, I probably would have chosen Mexican weather and exotic birds over Nebraska, too. Michael was uncertain. Curious about the cranes, he might well have been attracted by the strangeness of taking off three days to fly to Nebraska at a time when bad weather was likely. But it was an expensive and marginal sort of adventure and he, reasonably, had other priorities. I even tried to induce Marc, a friend of mine who grew up in Nebraska, and who actually loves the prairie, to join me (I had never met someone with that particular affection before). But while he really did want to go, his family responsibilities were much too great to allow such a rapid and frivolous visit. Poor Marge agreed to accompany me on the understanding that she didn't have to take part in all the birding activities.

But the winter proved crueler than our plans could sustain, and Marge's mother suffered a second attack which, after much agonizing, led to a quadruple bypass right around the time of the trip. I wasn't certain I should go, either, but Marge assured me that there would be no use in my missing out on the cranes while she spent most of her time at the hospital or tending to her mother's affairs—things that she had to do whether I was around or not. I suspect, in addition, she was more sensitive to my glumness than I was to the terrible difficulties of her winter. In any case, I allowed myself to be persuaded and so, booked for two, I singly flew off to Lincoln, Nebraska, in quest of the sandhill crane.

I knew I-80 as a long, tedious smoothly paved strip that evened out America from New Jersey to California, and Lincoln sat centrally on it. So did Grand Island. In a rented car, feeling odd about staying on that road for such a short time and stopping at a place that I had always in the past taken not as a goal but as just another landmark on the road to New York or California, I drove directly to a Grand Island Holiday Inn. I arrived in time for an orientation meeting of the Conservancy group, complete with film, informal lecture, personal introductions. These were my fellow craners for the next two days. Vince was director of the Nebraska Nature Conservancy, successfully putting on a public and social face when, even by the side of the slide projector, he was clearly a man who would be very comfortable out in the field. I believed immediately in his feeling for prairie habitat, for the people who cared about it, and of course for the work of the Conservancy out here.

He explained why it was that the cranes returned here every year and why it was that the sandhills thrived and whoopers didn't. Grand Island, a key point in the Platte River basin, was a perfect place for crustacean-eating migratory birds to fatten up on their way north, but with the transformations caused by agriculture, and particularly by the growing of corn, the crustaceans disappeared. The sandhills adapted, filled up on last year's corn, tons and tons of it, that was scattered prodigally in the surrounding fields, and flew north after a month of fattening. The whoopers did less well on the corn, but they still tended to fly into Grand Island for refueling, diminished though they were in numbers. Unfortunately for my visit, although I was prepared for the news, they arrived in April, just after the sandhills and long after I would have departed. But I was guaranteed more sandhills than I could possibly observe.

I was the only English professor in the bunch. It turns out, as Jane, one of the Conservancy guides told me, I was the only English professor who had ever come on this annual Nature Conservancy tour, and, ridiculously, I was a little proud of my uniqueness, a little disappointed in my profession. Feeling morally reinforced because I was supporting the Conservancy's excellent programs, I found it a difficult to admit that the programs could never have got me to Nebraska, only the birds. Jane, who took charge of organizational details, was alarmed to discover that though I had paid for two, I was only one. I suspected that the necessity of refund was worrying her, but she warmed to me quickly when—seeing how I might gain some birding advantages—I assured her that I would consider the money meant for Marge's participation a contribution to the Conservancy. A small price to pay, and anyway I got a receipt for tax purposes.

The plan was to gather in the late afternoon for a trip to some blinds at different spots on the river bank near the Platte mudflats where, at evening, the sandhills came to rest. We had two large vans, and I had already shifted my focus from New Jersey matters completely, feeling a kind of freshman excitement as I stepped in for the first session of my advanced education—in cranes. By the time we got to the blind, it was getting on to twilight. We had passed cranes, who were already becoming familiar, in small clusters pecking away in almost every surrounding field, but there was nothing on the Platte River but ducks, which I began to check with excitement. In my eagerness, I heard myself call "Shoveler," hoping perhaps to establish my birding credentials in this unfamiliar company. When nobody seemed to notice I let it go, beginning embarrassedly to recognize that the bird I was calling a shoveler was just a mallard. Later, Vince delicately made it clear that the shovelers did not arrive in these parts until further on in the season. Only a few of us had been paying attention to the ducks, and gradually, I became aware that Suzanne was an unusually sharp observer. Even in the gathering dusk she was finding interesting ducks and making quiet, interesting comments about them. Attracted as I am to people who know what they are doing around birds, I drifted over to her side. All of that, however, was prelude. I fairly quickly lost interest in the ducks and the large number of green winged teals that, under other circumstances, would have held my attention for a long and pleasurable time.

The others were watching the slow gathering of the cranes. As we moved toward darkness, the cranes, who had been scattered for miles around the river, began to move closer into adjoining fields and their voices seemed to be growing louder. There were hundreds of them a quarter mile in every direction, but the mudflats remained bare. Casually, apparently unsystematically, small and large flocks staged closer to the flats, seeming not to want to announce their real object and unwilling to get there until the last moment, but slowly making me aware that the sky was always full of the long graceful gliding birds. Watching intently, knowing what was coming, I nevertheless could not prepare myself for the sheer abundance: the air was full of cranes, everywhere, their high gobbling noise (Peterson's "garooo-a-a-a" doesn't do it justice) intensifying; the margins of the river were lost in cranes.

And the cranes were joined by the familiar honking of Canada geese and the "loud resonant choral *whouck* of the snow geese." Deep into twilight, we realized that we were being overwhelmed with sound, that it was not only outside us but rising within our own bodies, the honking and whoucking of geese, the gobbling of cranes. The reluctant birds gradually but without stop began to crowd each other noisily onto the flats. Ironically, amidst all that noise, we had to remain almost entirely silent, the slightest human sound from these innocuous blinds likely to drive the birds away, disturb their rest, ruin their migration, cut back on their breeding. We were to resist our own presence, only to watch and to hear. We were to do nothing and we could talk only in whispers. As the sound swelled so intensely that it was difficult to think of it as crescendo any longer, there was still plenty of room out there on the mud flats. Only a few hundred cranes and geese had moved in from the fields and the river margins as the others gathered at various distances. But gradually we understood that every inch of mud would soon be covered with geese in their spots, cranes standing tall, bustle to bustle, in theirs, all filling the air with oral notice of their presence. They came endlessly, it seemed—by the dozens, by the hundreds, small groups and large, not one of them silent, until we could only hear and feel them and in the gathering darkness sense that we were among them.

Yet each of those hundreds of thousands of cranes and geese, lost in the anonymity of their profusion, was an individual bird with its individual call, and Suzanne, listening intently, asked if I could detect, in the midst of the din, a passerine-like voice emerging from the gobbling crescendo. Almost as thrilling as the volume of sound was the experience of picking out from that volume, at Suzanne's prompting, an occasional individual high-pitched call that, she assured me, was the voice of a young crane. It took intense concentration to hear it, but the sound was there, and out among those gathering masses of birds on the mud flats, the young were joining the chorus.

I didn't know which I admired most, Suzanne listening or the cranes individually marking their places. Clearly, the power of that sound was registering on her as it was on me, the wonder of the recognition that all of it was no single sound at all but the conglomerate of separate striving voices, enormous, graceful, living creatures whose private lives we were here privileged to observe on the condition that we not disturb them; they did not know we were here. I have never heard such sound before, never felt so powerfully the vibrancy, abundance, raw force of life. Those hundreds of thousands of voices produced a cacophony entirely musical, transcending what we could see as darkness dimmed out those thriving burgeoning flats.

Vince, who had seen and heard this kind of gathering hundreds of times, knew its effect. We walked slowly away, talking about it softly, almost reverently, and in the darkness Vince, who seemed utterly at home in Nebraska and the prairies and the mud flats, pointed to the skies and mapped the constellations for us and almost, for a moment, made us feel at home in the world.

It was difficult for me, feeling newly alive and almost serene, to imagine anything better, but in the morning, we drove out to another blind, at another spot in the river, and watched in the growing light those mud flats now invisible beneath the teeming birds, and the sound rose once again. We were expecting something dramatic, but in fact, the cranes did it all quite casually and left as they had come, in small groups and large, and while the scene was impressive, it seemed unlikely that the diminishment could match the previous night's gathering. But as the emerging flats slowly became visible, we noticed from across the river a large dark form rise from the trees and soar toward us. It was calling, a high-pitched cry less regal than its size and flight. The bald eagle settled in a tree a few yards from us and was joined quickly by another. In other birding contexts, that would have been a triumphant moment, and it was, indeed, triumphant, as I watched those powerful birds closely. The eagles, who eventually numbered three, would, I thought, be the highlight of the morning. But shortly after, on a mudflat covered with thousands of Canada geese, honking notoriously and egregiously into the morning air, there fell a sudden silence. It seemed to last for a long time, eerily, but it couldn't have been more than two seconds. Then there was what seemed like an explosion, several thousand geese simultaneously leaping from the mud. Within seconds, there was no goose in sight, the mud flats were as bare as they had been the evening before.

To be thrilled by Canada geese, whose excrement fills the walkways of our local park and who graze aggressively on every open grassy field in New Jersey, was something I had not expected. Nobody could have convinced me, even minutes before, that the geese would have been more exciting than the eagles visible clearly with naked eye outside the blind. Those two seconds of silence, however, and the startling explosion of geese, by themselves justified my November decision.

We hadn't slept much, for good birding trips take you deep into the evening and start again before dawn. Exhilarated from the morning's experience, I still welcomed the brief break before our afternoon trip out to the Rainwater Basin for the waterfowl. The motel had packed a lunch but I was insatiable for birds, fantasizing about more ducks and possible waders. I took the risk of lying down in my room for fifteen minutes before the scheduled departure and I awoke more than a half hour later. Flushing like a kid late for class, I pulled on my boots, and clomped quickly to the buses. But they were gone: Vince, Suzanne, Jane and the whole group of craners had left without me. At first I was ashamed that I had allowed fatigue to catch up with me, and then I was angry that they hadn't even called the room, and then, remembering perhaps those sensations of November, I grew morose.

Here I was again invisible, incompetent, not strong enough to keep up with a group doing the thing I had spent all winter dreaming about and wishing to do. The letdown after the morning's bird high was intense. I got into my rented car and drove around the area, looking for the Rainwater Basin, getting inadequate instructions about how to find it. There were cranes standing in every field and I tried to rouse myself into excitement at seeing them. But my sense that I did not count, that my absence wasn't even noted, that my powers were dwindling, that I was stupidly alone in the middle of Nebraska with nowhere to go, nothing to do, got the better of me and I turned back to my room not even looking, the last five miles or so, at the cranes grazing for last year's corn.

In the evening explanations were good. I didn't know how I would address the young people whom I had so much admired the day before and during the morning with the eagles, geese, and cranes. But they made it easy because when they learned I hadn't been to the Rainwater Basin they were obviously shocked. Each bus noticed that I wasn't there; Jane and Suzanne, separately, assumed I was in the other bus. Okay. But the loss was irrevocable, except that when they and Vince learned that I would not be leaving immediately after the prairie chickens on the following morning, they volunteered to take me out to the Basin by myself as soon as the Conservancy tour was over. We talked about what they had seen, what I was likely to see, about birds and, of all things, Darwin. Suzanne was surprised to learn that an English professor might know something about Darwin who was, after all, a scientist, and asked me to recommend a good biography of him. Her interests in the natural world had taken her back to Darwin and so I told her about the various Darwin biographies I knew, finally recommending the recent one by Adrian Desmond and James Moore (which I had reviewed), and warning her of its biases and limitations. The connection between Darwin and the birds was easy.

We carried the discussion into the next day, which began in the chill quiet of a Nebraska predawn. By now I was assuming that Vince would produce what he promised, and as I sat agitated and silent in the cold dark of the bus, listening for a sound the brochure called "booming," I didn't know what I was listening for, but I was confident I would hear it. I barely picked up the sound at first, but silhouettes soon began to appear on the ridges against the horizon. Like most birds in the families of grouse and quail, the prairie chicken has something just a little silly about it, hugging the ground, flurrying with tails erect and rapid movement of the legs. I wouldn't have called the voice "booming": it was low, stretched out, almost like cooing, or as the National Geographic guide puts it, like "the sound made by blowing across the top of an empty bottle." So the prairie chickens really were out there, booming in their rather subdued ways, puffing their stunning yellow cheeks (which I could only see later when the sun was thoroughly up), cocking their tails, performing past the dawn on the top of low nearby ridges in the flat prairie setting that made Nebraska, and cheering me back into a surreptitious lifebird dance.

It was one of the bright mornings of my birding life, in part because I knew the prairie chickens were not to be the last of the day's birding pleasures. When the other craners had gone from Grand Island, I climbed into the van that Vince was driving, and with Suzanne and Jane we drove out to the Rainwater Basin while I heard what there was to know of the gossip of the Nebraska Nature Conservancy. As we chatted about Darwin, birds, the prairie, I felt entirely at home out on the prairie and among friends who were there because it was a pleasure for them to be there. Diverse as we were, the senior literature professor, the director of the Nature Conservancy (anthropologist, naturalist, fund-raiser), the two naturalist women who spent their lives working for the Conservancy and out in the fields whenever they could, we made a happily congenial group. There were gentle in-jokes at the expense of other Conservancy people and casually knowledgeable comments about the land and the water around us.

Out in the basin there were of course more birds: we found blue-winged teal and ring-necked ducks and an abundance of snow geese entirely filling the field of my binoculars. I was quietly impressed by the fact that my companions, who had just spent two days with the responsibility of leading duffers out into the field, were taking an entirely unfeigned pleasure in being here again even after the tours they were guiding were over. The snow geese were whoucking and circling. There was an occasional hawk over head. The sun was bright and the talk was about saving the land.

The pleasures of birding, with its intensities of gobbling cranes and eagles screaming and geese like snow across the entire field of my vision, are almost always also human pleasures. That afternoon in the Rainwater Basin brought together for me the thrilling vitality of the bird life I had come to observe with the quiet friendship that grows in the community of those who care about that life. Together, the birds and the people who love them put me in touch with the earth in a way that makes possible my imagination of it as home. The birds had brought me to the prairies of Nebraska, which my friend Marc had claimed (mysteriously to me) to love, had put me in touch with Suzanne, who could distinguish a young crane from hundreds of thousands of others gobbling into the dusk, and with Vince, who, I discovered, had begun learning the world he showed me as an undergraduate at Indiana University when I had taught there in the late 1960s.

These prairies harbor life everywhere, in their flatness and subtle rises, in the sweeping of their grasses, in the abundance of their birds. There is room out there to breathe and to map the stars, to feel long silences, and to watch the nuances of shape and color and form, unlike the sublimities of the Rockies yet almost sublime in their quiet vastness. Of course, those prairies are linked in memory with the babel of goose and crane intensifying that March evening into darkness, and that explosion of life off the flats, the banality of geese contending with the grace and power of eagles.

Suzanne has since written to say how much she enjoyed meeting me and hoping she could stop over in New Jersey with her husband for some birding adventures here. When I left Grand Island, she and Jane agreed that they wanted an English professor along on every crane tour. And when I returned to New Jersey, my mother-in-law was doing remarkably well.

greater roadrunner

ROADRUNNER

I GREW UP with Roadrunner cartoons and with the image of that manic, long-tailed, incongruously earthbound bird, legs spinning to a propeller blur and then zooming across the screen at superavian speed. So wonderfully appropriate for cartoon representation, it might well have been purely imaginary. But it turns out that there are such birds as roadrunners, and that they are fairly common in the Southwest. Unfortunately, I had never been to the Southwest. Like all pleasures long deferred, the roadrunner lived enticingly in my imagination. It seemed to me an exotic, even romantic creature, despite its early cartoon associations. Thanks to Peterson and other field guides, I had a clear sense of what it looked like, could see why it was so eligible for cartoons and yet why it would be so remarkable out in the desert. Part of the excitement of the anticipation was that I knew I could only see it by traveling to places I had never been. For many of my friends, however, most of whom had no interest in birds at all, the roadrunner was commonplace. Of course, I've seen roadrunners, they would tell me. Haven't you?

Well, no. And so the roadrunner became one of those birds I simply had to see and I thought longingly of it in the more regal company of unseen peregrine falcons and snowy owls. My best chance at a roadrunner would be on a visit to my brother, who owned a house in Palm Springs, where he spent several weeks each December and January. He had invited Marge and me out for a visit any time we could make it, and we knew, one recent December, that we would be in San Francisco for a conference. It made sense to travel from there down to Palm Springs, where I had never been, and which had always seemed to me the artificial and glitzy home of Bob Hope, Dinah Shore, and lots of glamour. What more appropriate place for a bird that had long starred in films.

My brother, who as a teenager was passionate for nature, who studied to be a wildlife conservationist with Aldo Leopold, and who risked frostbite in the marshes of Queens before Kennedy Airport (née Idlewild) was built, had become an unusually successful insurance man, running his own company, traveling around the world as a much solicited speaker on insurance matters. With the enormous energy, confidence and ambition that was to mark his career after a rather shaky start in which he had to reimagine himself and his relation to the past, he settled in comfortably with the Palm Springs rich and famous. Suspicious and ironic about such moves and such wealth, I was nevertheless curious to see Palm Springs, to see my brother's house, in fact, to see my brother. If part of my willingness to pay a visit had to do with the fact that my brother, while no longer an active "birder," was still much more knowledgeable than I and much more likely to be able to find them, the other part, perhaps equally strong, was that he and I—as utterly different as two brothers could be—needed each other, loved each other in our ways, bore with us the childhoods our now dead parents had given us. We were the family.

He was my big brother and he remains so, although I am about five inches taller than he. He is richer, more powerful, more decisive, more willing to take risks, and when I'm with him I find it easy to slide back into that childhood sense of dependence and helplessness that I had found inescapable with my parents, even when I was forty-five and a relatively big operator in my little world. My brother had always seemed to me to move in a much bigger world. On the wall of his study is a map of that world pocked with colored pins marking the places he has visited as invited (and well-paid) guest. There aren't many pinless spots, and since my parents' deaths I have been most likely to talk to him when he calls me from Kennedy, where he waits in the executive lounge for a flight to or from Australia, South Africa, China, Turkey, or points east, north, south, or west. There is a touch of filial affection in his voice all the time, and a touch (maybe I'm just inventing it) of condescension. Although there's no doubt he's proud of his kid brother for doing so well in a field that required few risks and offered relatively small rewards, I don't think he believes that I have had to work very hard on the way, and willingness to work hard is perhaps his highest criterion for the moral life.

This kind of relationship would seem not to bode well for satisfying visits, but I am always surprised when he and his wife, Sandy, and Marge and I get together. There is every reason to expect tensions and hostilities, as our differences on everything from how to bring up kids to how to run the government are extravagant. But we have a good time. He and Sandy are almost invariably warm and I think more than ostensibly happy to be with us. We talk deep into the night about family and our own activities, and we tend to step back from danger points as soon as we sense them. The day of my mother's funeral, peeing in an adjoining urinal, he was the one who broke through fifty years of austere and manly silence—the characteristic mode for my father as well as for his children—by telling me how moved he was by our connection and how much he cared for me. And it was he who picked up something that flashed through my mind at the moment and that I wouldn't have had the nerve to say, that it was lucky for our affection that we didn't live very near each other because our differences were too great for sustained contact.

That was right—both the warmth and the distance. But we could connect over childhood, children, grandchildren, and now birds. He was pleased and surprised by my belated interest. His interest in wildlife remains alive, although he tends to have even less time for the birds than I do. My visit might allow him to indulge that interest overtly, to find time from a work life that is constant and intense, though absolutely necessary to his psychological well-being. Last year, I entered a membership for him in the American Birding Association, and he has used it more effectively than I use mine. As he travels around the country and the world, he consults the Association's directory to contact people who might be willing to advise or guide him in areas he is about to visit, and he has reported some splendid birding experiences as a consequence, experiences which, needless to say, I in my more restricted travels envy. (We share the habit of attempting to turn every business trip into a birding trip as well.) Envy or not, we talk comfortably, happily about birds. And in preparation for our Palm Springs visit, Norman had assured me that he would find me a roadrunner.

I had my doubts. Promises of birds to be seen are only very occasionally fulfilled. It is part of the pleasure of birding that while birds are on the whole predictable, they are rarely predictable in the particular. The swallows en masse do come back to Capistrano when they're supposed to, and the cranes do turn up at Grand Island. Yet roadrunners might be common in an area and just happen not to be there when you are looking for them. One of the most impressive of my birding experiences was on a trip in which my ornithologist friend

Wade promised me an upland sandpiper, predicting that once we came over a slight rise in the midst of open New Jersey fields not much more than ten miles from my house, I would find one. Over the rise, there it was, standing solitary and unmistakable. Of course, Wade was taking a risk, going on his previous experiences in that place and hoping that the bird would stay true to form. It did, and that was my life "uppie," a bird probably much more difficult to find than the roadrunner. Wade knew he could be wrong, and I knew my brother might not find the birds he usually found, but it would be fun looking and missing, almost as much fun as looking and finding. And anyway, it was going to happen in Palm Springs.

Whether a bird is rare or common depends on many things besides whether there are a lot or a few of them. Rarity and commonness are oddly interchangeable qualities in birdland. The fulmar, perhaps one of the most populous bird species in the world, a stiff-winged gull-like ocean flyer, would certainly set off the rare bird alert if it were spotted, as I have never spotted it, immediately off the coast of New Jersey or New York. Yet when I visited Scotland at some ruins by the shore near St. Andrew's, fulmars were everywhere. Similarly, driving across this country, birders will note that the cardinal disappears somewhere west of the Mississippi, though it is common even in my backyard. When we got to Palm Springs, one of the first things Norman pointed out to me was a phainopepla, sitting in a tree in his back yard. I remembered the bird from the field guides because of the oddness of its name, but of course I had never seen one. Norman's backyard bird was for me a "lifer," and I should have done my lifebird dance there. The phainopepla looks sort of like a black cardinal, but it's flycatcher not finch related. The very idea of the rare bird —say, the famous Ross's gull spotted in Massachusetts some years ago—is almost entirely a question of geography. Birds tend to hang out in predictable places. When they move to other places, they are called "rare."

The spotted redshank, for instance, became notorious when it was identified on a dilapidated wharf in an obscure section of Brooklyn. The idea of rarity seemed peculiarly odd in this case, not only because the bird is not at all rare in Europe, where it belongs, but because of the distinctly unromantic and public conditions in which it located itself here. The redshank was a bird Paul, Michael, and I thought it was worth detouring to find. We had heard of it on the New York rare bird alert, and on the day of our annual spring outing, it made sense for us to drive through Brooklyn and see if we could spot it as well. The hard part was finding the exact address, but as we angled through the streets toward Avenue X, we knew we were home when we saw a block away a parking lot near the water where forty or fifty people, all equipped with spotting scopes and binoculars, were standing, for the most part chatting, with a few aiming their scopes at the ruined wharf where gulls, shorebirds, and cormorants were all sitting. It was a giant party. Everyone was there for the redshank; everyone was swapping bird stories. Some few were giving advice to newcomers about where on the decaying timbers the redshank was standing. It was visible to the naked eye quite comfortably, even to my naked eye, yet the scope was still slow to provide me with the clues that would distinguish it from the greater yellowlegs that was standing right next to it. When I first saw it, it was standing on one leg, head tucked in. But the leg was red not yellow, and there was plenty of time for looking. That bird had been there not hours but days. It was undisturbed by its audience. We gave it more than fifteen minutes, not only so that we could see all its field marks—the body, even not in breeding plumage, was darker than the yellowlegs's, and its bill drooped slightly at the end—but because the anthropology of the birding community there was irresistibly interesting and comic. Michael loved it, but after the first minutes of serious looking and distinguishing of field marks, it was hardly birding we were doing. The "rarity" made itself too casually available to allow us to feel that it was rare and when we left, it had not moved from the spot in which we found it.

But the roadrunner was certainly rare to me when we arrived at my brother's place in Palm Springs, an adobe-style house surprisingly like the rest of the houses visible from it. My brother's backyard, with its fruited orange and grapefruit trees and its swimming pool, became a brief birder's paradise for me. Bushtits, verdin, and other California commonplaces were thrilling to my Eastern eyes, and Norman knew it and encouraged my pleasure. Even as I continued to check every movement through my binoculars, watching for the sudden rustling of leaves in my brother's and his neighbors' trees, we began to talk about taking a serious birding trip. We didn't really ask our wives, Marge, who could live without birds but loved landscape, and Sandy, who had very little of the naturalist in her. They, however, were immediately agreeable, Marge because she wanted to see the landscape and because under the terms of this visit she had acquiesced in family compromises, Sandy because her highest priority is always family. In any case, Norman's backyard had already justified the trip, from the standpoint of birding; a ride to the Salton Sea would be a happy bonus.

That ride didn't turn up the roadrunner, although it did yield a remarkable abundance of ducks, geese, egrets, and shore birds. In a very short time, we spotted thirty-eight species of birds, snow geese in Disney-like numbers, green-winged and cinnamon teals, grebes, a lifebird towhee—the Abert's—stilts and avocets, and water pipits, and shrikes, and more. It was, nevertheless, a very moderate bird outing, Sandy dressed not quite appropriately for the wilderness, Norman and I perhaps surprisingly sensitive to the levels of boredom and discomfort we might reasonably inflict on the women, who were being at least overtly tolerant but who were not much given to the sort of birding trivia that constitutes a large part of any birding trip and that fills the car when Paul, Michael, and I go out together. But I felt no tension and relaxed into the ease of the birding, the ease of the relationships. The trip was in fact a family outing, and entirely successful in that respect. That it managed to give us interesting sightings of so many birds simply whetted my appetite for a more serious birding venture in which we could work hard to find what was not immediately visible and move into territory that required more rugged costume. We returned, pleased with the day but with no roadrunner to add to my birding experience.

The rest of the visit passed without even moderately serious birding. We got a look at the monstrously incongruous desert hotel that opens in its lobby into a set of canals and that is islanded in an artificial lagoon so that one can take a boat to one's room. The lavish and wildly inappropriate expenditure of water, which I have to confess impressed me precisely as I expect it was supposed to impress anyone who saw it, seemed somehow more accurately an indication of the kind of place Palm Springs is than a roadrunner might have been. Roadrunners, after all, don't spend a lot of time in the lake country. There were birds in the tropical setting of the hotel lobby, where exotic South American and African species had been imported to give a touch of Palm Springs authenticity to the place. I was eager to see them, eager to watch the movement and hear the sound of the water, guilty about being delighted. Unfortunately, artificially imported birds don't count on any respectable birder's list. Our visit to the hotel was not, in any case, to see birds; rather it was to contemplate a man-made wonder in which, by the way, my brother's financial company had made an early investment.

The last day before our departure, Norman was determined to find me a roadrunner after all. He recalled that my longed-for exotic species was commonly seen in the parking lot of one of his two country clubs, the one of which Dinah Shore was a member. So we took a chance and drove over there. The place had its interest, whether roadrunners showed up or not. It was the older of the two clubs but it was farther away from the house and a little inconvenient. It was also a little classier in tone if not obviously richer. The grounds, as one might have expected, were beautiful and green. There was a smartly groomed pond in which several species of ducks, not only mallards, were swimming.

We stopped for a while and walked around. No roadrunners but some pleasant conversation in some pleasant surroundings. At last, having agreed that we had to give up on the roadrunners and get back in the car and just about settling in, I heard my brother note in a rather casual voice, "There they are," and he pointed beyond some Mercedeses and Rolls Royces to the edge of the parking lot and a low wooden fence where three tall brownish birds, almost two feet long from bill to enormous tail, scooted casually in an out of the brush onto the parking lot pavement, their distinctively long tails sometimes cocked characteristically upward, long necks stretched forward.

The identification was immediate and required little birding expertise. A roadrunner is an unmistakable bird, brown though most of it is. And three roadrunners, scuttling among the cars and the bushes, are hard to miss. My brother's casual call suggested how easy they were to see, and how common a sight they were for him. So the sighting was about as undramatic and banal as an exotic lifebird could make it. The three walked as though they were not at all special and took the cars as a normal part of their lives. Here in the parking lot, they were no more out of place than the watery hotel in the desert. Intent on their quest for insects and other prey, they were in no hurry to leave and in no apparent fear of human harassment. It was easy to watch them—which we did—for many minutes. I had expected that I would find the birds, if I ever did, in arid, desert surroundings. Instead, these pedestrian cuckoos, close cousins to the much more secretive and romantic cuckoos who prefer flying to walking, were at ease in the world of Dinah Shore and duck ponds and fancy automobiles.

But my brother had produced, as promised. And I was grateful. This parking lot expedition was a gesture of affection and at the same time a mutual celebration of the erratic and unpredictable pleasures of the birding life. I had a new lifebird and could, the next day, set out for New Jersey, three thousand miles from my brother's winter home, where sight of a road-runner would once again be impossible and I would await the next phone call from some executive lounge of Kennedy.

peregrine falcon

SHARPIE

*R*APTORS are birds that non-birders know and feel strongly about. They are birds about which it is impossible not to feel strongly. At the top of the avian food chain, they are powerful and graceful killers, and what they kill is conspicuous. Gnatcatchers eat gnats, and swallows catch in their erratic flights all sorts of insects, and flycatchers, of course, catch flies—among other things. But a peregrine falcon, in its powerful stoop, descending at speeds that make it quite literally inescapable and exploding into a pigeon in a storm of feathers, demands attention. Even the gentlest of birders is likely to wish for that breathtaking moment of violence, of the sort I saw the other day in Jamaica Bay, when a peregrine I didn't know was there suddenly took a desperate wigeon in a burst of feathers, and a pond full of ducks emptied in seconds.

The peregrine is one of the largest of our falcons, and the fastest, and its powers are greater than those of most of the other hawks. But a crooked-winged osprey, almost eagle size, diving from high above a tidal pond, then struggling out of the water with a fish in its talons is hardly less astonishing and impressive. Our garbage dumps are filled with red-tailed hawks who feed on the rats and sit or fly majestically, almost eagle-like, identifiable at last both by their distinctive "buteo" shape—broad-winged, broad-tailed—and by the flash of rufous tail. Every raptor, even the vultures that don't kill but wait for our roadside killings or other forms of premature death, are beautiful in their way. Close up, the turkey vulture might be taken as grotesque, with its massive black body and small red featherless head, but in the air, wobbling slightly in its shallow "V" flight, it has a grace that makes its long thin wings regal in their control.

Raptors do take my breath away. Our smallest raptor, the kestrel, is a lovely falcon, with reddish back and blue wings and deep sideburns on its white face, but it is only about the size of a blue jay. That is, until it moves in flight, its pointed wings cutting the air and making it seem twice as large, more than twice as powerful. Its relative commonness—sitting deceptively silhouetted, almost pudgy from a distance, with a thin tail extending down—does nothing to diminish the felt intensity of its presence, its almost gaudy contrast of reds and blues when seen close up, the acrobatic virtuosity of its skills. The kestrel was the first bird I identified by virtue of its behavior rather than its color or shape. It was an early day in my birding life and I was emerging from a nearby woods excited by what I had managed to see so near home when, over the adjoining fields, I caught a bird leaning on the rolling air, which held level underneath him, wings moving rapidly but without haste, back slightly arched as if to allow it to see the earth more clearly, and no other movement. It hung there, leaning against an invisible podium, and my breath came short. There was Hopkins's "Windhover" doing what I had only heard kestrels did, and doing it with a mastery that—

even after twenty years of watching such displays—still makes me gasp.

Hummingbirds hover, too, and hang immobile at a flower's lip while their wings beat with insect-like rapidity barely visible to the eye. Beautiful in its own miraculous way, the hummingbird, however, doesn't make me gasp. I love hummingbirds almost as much as I do hawks, but hawks in their size and power and apparent calm, as they soar or hover or gyre into an ultimately invisible distance, inspire an awe and envy that smaller birds can't. The great birds are often harried by smaller ones, but when I see blackbirds going at hawks, for instance, diving relentlessly at them in midair and driving them away from their territories, that is one time I am on the side of the big guy. The little chattering birds, even the noisy attacking crows, seem so petty, so rough and awkward in their flights that I often find myself wishing the hawks would simply rip one of the offenders out of the air. More satisfying yet is watching a hawk or, better, an eagle, attacked higher into the sky by the smaller birds, finally gliding up and away beyond their reach, barely flapping a dignified wing as the others hectically strain, with rapid wingbeats, to catch up.

The extraordinary dignity and power of these birds came home early and indelibly to me on a trip to Hawk Mountain. It was the first time I went there, to this remarkable spot in the Alleghenies from which you can watch a very large proportion of the south-migrating raptors as they sweep from one mountain to another across well-groomed Pennsylvania valleys below. My brother had decided that he and his wife would take me and Marge, my mother and father to see the mountain one very mild autumn day. It was an early sign of my father's declining health, for halfway up from the parking lot, he knew that it wasn't a good idea for him to continue. We all thought it was a moment when we would have to give up on the birds, but he was okay, only being cautious, and urged us to continue without him. We did continue, hiking up to the North Lookout, from where you can see across a broad and lovely farmer's valley a distant mountain with five distinctly visible crests, each of which the birders numbered and used as reference points for their sightings. "Osprey over four," someone would remark about a bird that was certainly more than a mile away and that I could only make out as a speck over the last crest but one to the right. "Cooper's over three." "Golden eagle over two."

In fact, the moment we arrived at the North lookout someone made such a call. I looked eagerly at "two" and could make out a distinctly large and impressive bird soaring flatwinged in our direction, although even as it approached middle distance I wouldn't have dared to name it. As it moved closer, I held it in my binoculars, catching the very occasional wingbeat, beginning to get a sense of texture and color. It got close enough that I seemed to hear the wind through its wings as it came at us, virtually at eye level and then slowly took an upcurrent. Dark all through its body, and with a clearly banded tail, it was certainly (so the experts were saying) a mature bird. Mature or not, it gave a spacious sense of ease in the world that made me hold my breath. It seemed enormous, its seven or eight foot wingspan filling my glasses as it gyred slowly above us. That sighting, as it hung above me on the wind, was probably the best I would ever have of a golden eagle. The gyre widened, the bird, without a movement of its wings, began to recede into the heights above us, taking the currents as high as it could until, by that time, almost out of sight even through binoculars, it could glide downward for miles and miles effortlessly to wherever golden eagles go when they migrate through the Alleghenies. I was sorry that my father had remained below.

The serendipity of those first moments on the North Lookout made me assume that this kind of thing was commonplace up there. In other visits to Hawk Mountain, sometimes with Marge, but usually with Paul, I have had to sit through long hours of hawkless skies, entertained only by the loveliness of the site and by the continuing chatter of birders, skilled and ignorant, as they sprawled over the rocks, munched their sandwiches, kept their eyes always on those crests from which the hawks almost invariably came. Usually, however, the waits will have been worth it. In the early stages of fall migration, broadwinged hawks—perhaps the weakest flyers of the buteos—come through in numbers that would have seemed more appropriate to starlings. Broadwings often "kettle," or converge in vast circles of hawks, in numbers higher than one can count, and spin slowly above as they mass into the warm air currents that will allow them to glide unstrained to the south with as little beating of the wings as possible. Even the "weakest" of the raptors evokes imagination of effortless control.

The smallest of the accipiters, described by Peterson as "longtailed hawks with short rounded wings," is the sharp-shinned hawk. It too appears in great numbers over the ridges at Hawk Mountain. Although it seems much larger, the male "sharpie" is not much bigger than the purple grackle. But it is distinctly a hawk, and it has a characteristic flight—flap flap soar, Paul and I describe it, flap flap soar. At a distance it is, for me, just about impossible to tell it from a cooper's hawk, which has essentially the same shape and markings but is on the whole a few inches larger. Although books tell you that the male sharpie's tail is flat and slightly notched, the cooper's more rounded, it is all but impossible to make even much larger distinctions of birds flying by at stunning speeds more than a quarter mile away and bending in the wind. In fact, raptors are often extremely difficult to identify. Usually they are spotted at some distance as they soar above the roads or woods or fields, and the marks one looks for are sometimes smaller than an inch. Even the grossest distinctions between buteo and accipiter families can be problematic if the birds are flying into a strong wind. One of the reasons Hawk Mountain is such a good place to be for raptor migration is that one can always count on the presence of a large number of real experts, even official recorders of the hawk flights. Just about every hawk that passes the mountain during migration season gets censused and recorded, and officials of the Hawk Mountain association are in constant contact from the North and South Lookouts. Eavesdropping amateurs like me quickly find out what the smallest speck in the sky is, and after a while, as almost every distant identification is confirmed when the bird gets within naked eyeshot, always believe.

Hawk Mountain is a place for special-occasion hawk-watching. But anyone with eyes at the ready will find hawks around in places one would never, as an amateur, suspect. I used to join the January raptor count in my area, and was assigned a strip roughly along Route 1, from New Brunswick down past Princeton. There, in some of the few remaining trees, or just back off the road in wooded stands fully visible to all the commuters, or on small farms not far from the main road, or on telephone wires anywhere near where a vole or rat or mouse might pass, would be red tails, and kestrels, and northern harriers (marsh hawks) and occasional rough-legs, and certainly turkey vultures.

The sharp-shinned hawk is one of the more common raptors in my area, but I don't see it very often. Although hawks are common enough in many places, they are not everyday occurrences for people whose lives are not dedicated to birding. Hawks continue to feel to me like birds that mark a radical distinction between the domestic, the urban or suburban, and the "natural." Knowing how problematic that idea of the "natural" can be, I still hold in my head a false but common-sense notion of a world largely undisturbed by human development, and the hawks mark for me the space where that world most distinctly begins. It's not only their power and control, but it's the apparent ease with which they move over vast spaces, and the dignity of their movements—the peregrine diving, the eagle soaring, the kestrel hovering.

They are not, that is to say, backyard birds, especially if your backyard is a small suburban lot, big enough for a few bushes, not big enough for a single "dwarf" apple tree that had grown to the height of the roof and whose branches threatened to enter the bathroom. That tree had to come down a few years ago so that we could see the yard. I was sorry, because in the spring when it was beginning to leaf I not infrequently sat on my toilet and spotted Tennessee warblers, or blackpolls, or redstarts in the treetop, and because it irregularly drew yellow-bellied sapsuckers to its wide and pockmarked trunk. Once the tree was down, my autumn-winter birdfeeding became less successful.

In the fall last year, as I set up my feeder for the winter, I determined to increase the bird-seductiveness of my yard. From an almost squirrel-proof line I stretched across from the garage to a pipe outside my kitchen window, I hung two tubular feeders, one with sunflower seed, one with "thistle" seed, and a suet cage. It was smorgasbord intended to attract anything that could fly and was hungry. And in the first weeks of the fall, as the cold began to settle in seriously, the feeders were far more successful than my single feeder had been in preceding years. The suet brought a downy woodpecker family, male and female, and red-breasted nuthatches and white-breasted nuthatches and, with some frequency, a Carolina wren. The thistle seed was working for the goldfinches, which were still brilliant yellow when they began feeding but fairly quickly went olive and drab. The noisy and growing population of house finches dominated the sunflower seed, although chickadees and titmice always did well. Pine siskins also began to arrive, and that was really cheering for me. The yard was thick and messy with bird seeds and sunflower husks, in which cardinals, mourning doves, juncos, song sparrows, and white-throated sparrows kicked and scraped for food.

Marge has always liked the feeder although neither she nor I is wild about the mess on the ground that grows inches thick through the winter and needs serious shoveling out in the spring. Making coffee in the morning, I would report what was going on out there. She would always tell me if anything strange turned up. Here was our one mutually satisfying bird-watching territory. Marge indulged my passion and the binoculars that I sometimes forgot to take away from the kitchen sink, as she had indulged the happy absurdity of our telephone, a duck that quacks instead of rings, and whose eyes light up when it is being used. It's an ugly and an awkward thing, and Marge is an artist who cares a lot more about the nature of the objects and design around her than I. But she gives me my birds and only repents when, after reporting a strange sighting, I bombard her with detailed questions about bill-size, markings on the wing, shape of the tail, and so on. Now she prefaces each bird note with, "Don't ask me any more questions about it. This is all I saw." And I badger her with only a few.

The year of our first visit from redpolls, we had an outdoor cat. The morning a redpoll arrived, I was ecstatic. It was a lifebird for me, and I watched it until I was almost late for work. I gabbled about it to Marge endlessly. In the afternoon, as I sat at my desk, I got an elegiac call from Marge: "What did that bird look like? Did it have a red patch on the front of its head?" I was stunned and barely had time to think about how the call represented Marge's real concern for me and my bird indulgences. I had read that redpolls are as comfortable with people as chickadees, as unsuspicious. This one was insufficiently suspicious of the cat. It was a dark day at home, and Marge was full of comic consolation. But it turned out after all that the winter was horrendous, and redpolls became regulars at the feeder without any further mishaps.

This year looked as feeder-rich as that one had been, and Marge was again touchingly patient with my constant talk about bird activity in the yard. Each morning I would go out jogging very early and return, sweaty and happily uncomfortable, to a yard full of chirping and feeding activity. Without hesitation I would take my last paces into the yard, and there would be a flurry at the feeder as the birds dispersed until the yard emptied again. Cooling down, I would walk around the house a few times, and go in to make coffee and see what else might come to the feeder that day.

As I came up the street for my final run into the yard, Marge suddenly burst from the front door and in a loud whisper stopped me: "There's a hawk in the backyard." My skepticism about Marge's birding skills is in excess of what is just. Not too long ago, at a country wedding, I noted a strange, light tannish downy feather, about an inch or two long, with some slight hint of dark striping. I wondered aloud what bird could produce that kind of feather, and Marge immediately said, "Grouse." Now I almost never see grouse, and I was amused at the audacity of Marge's call. "Of course not," I said. But it was indeed a grouse feather, and I'm not even sure Marge has ever seen a grouse. I was appropriately humbled, and I'm still puzzled about how she could have been right.

So when she called "hawk" and kept me from going into the backyard, I had my doubts. But I was not about to risk frightening away whatever bird it was. Often when such calls are made, the bird will have disappeared by the time anybody else arrives. I went to the back window quickly and as quietly as I could. The feeders were empty, and there in the lilac bush, usually a staging ground for birds ready to perch at the feeders, and no more than ten feet from the window, sat a hawk: erect, stern, concentrated, sharp-hooked beak clearly visible, yellow talons grasping the branch. I was eye to eye with a sharpie, as close as I had ever been to one.

There were no problems with identification here. The flat tail, the heavily marked breast, were unmistakable. It was a small hawk, but in that lilac tree it was powerful and dominant. No other bird was going to venture into my yard that morning. I could have kissed Marge for warning me, for knowing it was a hawk, for sharing with me the excitement of the visit, but of course I was too intently watching the yellowy eye of what was probably an immature bird. It was worth a season of feeding.

It was there, ironically enough, because my feeders had been so successful. Hawk breakfast was sitting on the perches of my feeding tubes, and the sharpie had undoubtedly dropped in to tear up and swallow at least one of those finches, or siskins, or chickadees. There were no bird feathers anywhere, and I had to assume that the sharpie had missed. Then, after a few silent minutes, it grew restless, showed some signs of getting ready to move, and took off, probably for some other backyard feeder.

Marge accuses me of being undemocratic in my birding. There are some birds I don't care about much, some I care about a lot. If something happens to a house sparrow or a starling, I'm not much disturbed. But the death of that redpoll was a blow. And here I was celebrating the presence in my yard of a killer, of a creature who was there only to kill one of the birds I had lured deliberately with my feeders. I did pay a price for that visit, one that I was not happy paying but that I would pay again: for weeks after the hawk's visit, my feeders stood almost unused. No siskins returned for the rest of the winter. Many of my birds abandoned the yard for other feeders a few houses down. A very dark winter followed and there weren't a lot of backyard birds to cheer me through it.

But the rules of bird life and birding aren't the same as those that govern my politics. I do care about hawks, the oppressors, more than I care about house finches or robins or grackles, their potential victims. I make no apologies. Just take a look at a hawk in the wild some day, even wild in the backyard, and it will be clear that no explanation is necessary and that a sharpie, vicious beaked, sharp taloned, sitting at the top of the bird food chain in a lilac bush, is probably worth more than a season of finches.

hooded warbler

HOODED

BIRDERS WEAR binoculars and buy a lot of optical equipment. Much of what they do when they bird is look. They are, in a way, the ultimate voyeurs, since success in their activity means seeing without being seen. Early in my birding career, on a family trip to Martha's Vineyard, I took my binoculars for a walk in areas unfamiliar to me, and stumbled happily among dunes and beach plums with the smell of ocean and the brightness of the holiday time, and with a rare sense of freedom to seek out the birds I didn't know along the shore. Moving into a fresh area, I climbed a steep dune beyond which, I knew, would be the ocean, and at the top I stood tall, legs apart, binoculars scanning the new beach. Wherever they moved they encountered not sandpipers and plovers, but bare breasts, bare bottoms, pubic hair, sagging bellies. I didn't know whether I had been observed observing, but I fled as quickly as I could down the dune and realized as I walked rapidly away how inevitable the interpretation of my actions and my binoculars would be.

Birders almost instinctively do all they can to keep the objects of their desires from knowing they are being watched. I'm not sure what the nudists would have done if they had seen me, but if the bird sees or even senses human presence, it is likely to fly away. One of the most difficult aspects of birding for me is the need to keep so edgily alert that I never climb a dune for a new perspective on the beach or round the bend of a woodsy path or break through the tangled underbrush or approach an open duck pond without muting my being, diminishing the inevitable noise and disruptions caused by my simple and inescapable physical presence. If I'm birding, I can't forget for long that I—whom I can't see and whose presence I tend to discount—am taking up space, visible, tangible, noisy, a threat to something that lives there. I have missed hundreds of birds because for an instant I relaxed into unselfconsciousness about the ways in which even the gentlest walking sets up disturbances all around me. Alarmed by my body as they were feeding on the side of the path or in a low bush or a few yards out on the water, birds have darted away too fast for me even to guess at what they are. There are, of course, birds that don't mind so much: putting aside those egregious urban pigeons, there are sweeter birds like the black-capped chickadee, for example, or the poor redpoll that didn't sufficiently distrust my cat, or those mallards and geese that are used to being fed at local ponds and that I am a little embarrassed to check off on my day lists because they might as well be in cages.

The voyeur's self-consciousness depends, however, on an ultimate unselfconsciousness, the failure to think of oneself as being watched while watching. As birders, Paul and I regularly played out our rituals of self diminishment for the sake of the pleasure of the birds we could come upon unawares. We dressed only in accordance with the weather and we dined in grungy places or out in the woods or by the shore, on hastily prepared sandwiches and overrich gorp. And we never thought about what we might look like to other people except where our birding brought us to the margins of private property and to the potential threat of nervous and possessive landowners.

That was the way it was until Michael entered our birding circle, Michael the anthropologist, birder, people watcher. He came as shabbily dressed as we and, in what might be thought of as his apprentice years, he acquiesced in our style of birding, although exerting increasing pressure to make the food better and warmer. We three voyeurs wandered the New York and New Jersey countryside looking for the birds with the sort of comfortable enthusiasm that makes birding not only a means to find one's way more happily through what is traditionally called "nature," but an ultimately very social pleasure. On one trip, after three days of birds and unshaven shabbiness, as we returned to civilization, Michael saw us all through the eyes of imagined spectators: "Dorks," was what he called us, and we laughed in acknowledgment.

Soon Michael was finding other ways to pull back from our birding habits. It's now all but certain that when the three of us go birding together, Michael will disappear for long periods, check out the fauna, seek what we miss, and end the day with an entirely different experience from ours. With a special sort of detachment, Michael makes us aware that buried in our mutualities and our affection for each other there is just a touch of competitiveness after all. He enjoys seeing species that Paul and I don't see. In any case, somehow, doing it on his own is more satisfying to him than the communal pleasures of birding that seem necessary for Paul and me. I am told by a mutual friend that when Michael went backpacking with him and other non-birders in the Rockies, he suddenly turned birder again and strayed off from the group in order to find some obscure bird that they would not have noticed or in which they wouldn't have been terribly interested.

By conscious choice, Michael stands outside, and in this respect he is my opposite. I am not by instinct a joiner but I am by desire. Nervous about the wilderness, I tend to stay on the paths and take the roads more traveled by, not only because I fear getting lost, or because I want to avoid things like wood and deer ticks, but because I have a probably unjustified trust in people's accumulated experience. From the start, Michael plunged into the underbrush, where I only occasionally followed him, but then closely. If we move left, he moves right. As Paul and I tend to stay together, taking pleasure in our mutual discoveries, Michael makes his discoveries on his own.

Unless, that is, his focus for the while is on the behavior of the birders. It might be fair to say that this concern with what the human participants are doing is central for Michael almost all the time. He takes pleasure in planning the trips and in talking them through with Paul. He takes pleasure in driving to the places he has planned for and joining in the pre-trip bird chat. And he takes pleasure in such recognitions as the "dorkiness" of our aspects and the ritual unselfconsciousness of our behavior. Yet not quite in spite of himself, Michael had become a pretty good birder, too. He had, with his usual almost obsessive energy for avocations, eccentricities, and weirdly interesting bypaths, taught himself more about birding in the first few months of the interest I imagine I had sparked in him than I had learned in ten years. While his eyes were worse than mine, he was far better in the woods and the wilderness, where he had been comfortable long before he met me.

If birds were new to him, the kinds of places were not. The birds gave him a reason to be out there, and I was surprised to discover that while the first time we went out together he was willing to venture that a mockingbird was a shrike (they do look a lot alike in the field guides), within a few months he was scaring me off difficult identifications, more like a skeptic than an enthusiast.

The skepticism belongs with his anthropological bent. Since his investment in the birders became larger than his investment in the birds, Michael also became, as it were, a voyeur of voyeurs. Several years ago on a Sunday morning a friend of mine called to ask about a piece he had just read in the New Jersey section of the *Times*. It was about a visit to an enormous local landfill by the writer and two friends, "the naturalist" and "the literary man." Were you, my friend asked, the "literary man"? Indeed I was. Michael had written a funny and lucid piece describing how Wade and I had joined him in spotting hawks, owls, and foxes amidst stench and surreal landscape. I was easily identifiable because, as my friend knew, a) I was a literary man; b) I tended to pick up pennies when I found them, and finding two pennies in the dump, I began talking about the valuable "dust heaps" in Dickens's *Our Mutual Friend*; c) I loved birds and would put up with a lot to find them. Michael, the anthropologist, participant-observer had turned me into a character (as I fear, Michael and Paul are becoming characters at my hands). This first public notice of my birding ventures had made me a mini-celebrity among my non-birding friends.

I was pleased to find myself a character to be observed, with my eccentricities and unselfconscious enthusiasms exposed to the New Jersey readers of the Sunday *Times*. But as the three of us went off on our infrequent but regular trips, it became increasingly difficult to forget that I was being watched, and that Michael had always been watching, as he had, I now remembered, on an early trip to Jamaica Bay during which Paul and I were finding what turned out to be my life Philadelphia vireo. More striking to me in retrospect than the observation of the Philadelphia vireo was the fact that we had become to Michael as interesting as the bird was to us. While Paul and I worked hard to avoid spooking the bird and at the same time to see it unmistakably as it skulked in a low bush, Michael lay on the grass, listening to us whispering field marks, watching our concentration and perhaps absurd seriousness as we made too subtle discriminations and worried about getting it right. It was odd to be aware that we were doing something odd, being almost ridiculously scrupulous in arriving at our conclusion. When Paul asked the inevitable question: "Are you satisfied that it's a Philadelphia, George?" and I was satisfied, Michael was learning our tribal rituals.

He was certainly one of us, but because he was, the idea of "one of us" changed some, and I had to realize without evasion that what Paul and I were doing for birding satisfaction was anthropologically peculiar. In effacing ourselves for the birds, we were affirming ourselves as members of a tribe, defining ourselves against certain mainstream aspects of our society, making ourselves characters and eccentrics. I felt no diminution in birding pleasures, but a certain unreflective austerity which had been, ironically, part of the pleasure did disappear. While he would go along with our most horrendous decisions to get up in the deep darkness of the small hours, Michael struggled for every possible fifteen minutes of additional rest. At Point Pelee, he took a break in the middle of the day to go back to the motel, for me an utterly unimaginable surrender. His concern with food, which was as interesting to him as the birds because there is certainly an anthropology of restaurants and because food tastes good, too, led us to new forms of ritual. For the most part we gave up our bad sandwiches in the wild for sometimes excessively long lunches that ate up some of the daylight we might have spent on birds. The highlight of the birding day for Michael often seemed to be the roundup dinner at some restaurant after dusk in an area not far from the birds. A few years after Michael joined us, our planning for trips began to entail investigation of the best eating places in the area. Michael's tendency to obsessive research on odd corners of knowledge will surely some day produce a guide to dining for birders. A dish of mussels with spicy marinara sauce that he discovered in an

Italian restaurant near Jamaica Bay has occupied as much time in conversation as most of the birds.

But voyeurism and even anthropological study entail a distance that often seems belied by the intensity of Michael's immediate obsessions. There's a lot to those obsessions that is not accessible even to his closest friends. His engagement with the world of birds, for example, extended into a touching relationship with a mockingbird chick he rescued, to which he became a mother, and whom I occasionally found sitting like Mr. Boythorn's canary on his shoulder, eating from his mouth. Michael learned all there was to learn about raising wild birds and brought up "Twerp," whose name suggests something of the ironies with which feeling can be buffered, in the manner of *Born Free*, knowing he had to release the grown bird into the wilds of Highland Park, New Jersey. That relationship was no joke, but just as Michael had turned me into the "literary man" for the *Times*, after a period of several years he produced an essay full of fine and self-critical complexity about himself and Twerp—always the participant-observer. However painful it may be for him, Michael seems unhappily aware that it's necessary to release each bird into the wild, and he's ready to do it. I am too anxious and ignorant to take care of abandoned birds; and I never have to release them.

Although he joined the natives effectively enough to make us occasionally forget that he was watching us, he only rarely gave himself to our enthusiasms. At the end of each birding day, formerly concluded in third-rate diners where Paul and I relished the totaling of our day's observations, Michael relished the good food he had found us and preferred watching us counting to counting itself. I can't remember whether he ever totaled up his sightings for the day, and he certainly has not done so for many years. So while every trip produced unselfconscious moments of birding engagement and self-effacement, Michael made us all aware, as he was aware from the start, that these birding trips were about much more than finding birds.

His inclination to watch led me to watch in new ways in return. My sense of myself as a birder was increasingly shaped by watching Michael watch me watch the birds. I also watched the friendship that grew up rapidly between Michael and Paul after I introduced them. Michael found in Paul a man who was not only unusually supportive in the quest for the birds despite his much longer experience and wider knowledge, but a broadly read and sympathetic friend whose wife's recent decision to split with him became important to Michael's sense of his own domestic instabilities. They both now know more about birds than I do; they both are better in the wild; they both have lived through broken marriages. Paul's capacity to open himself to other people's feelings, a quality that helps make him a good birder, clearly touched Michael and has continued to matter to him. So while Michael became a legitimate and, in his ironic way, enthusiastic participant in our trips, he confessed that his interest in the birds themselves had diminished: it didn't, in the end, matter too much to him whether he could identify any given bird. It didn't matter too much that he failed to see some of the birds that made Paul and me unreasonably happy. He was pleased rather to watch us be unreasonably happy.

Several years after watching Michael and Twerp, I watched him with the young and fatherless Sasha. That relationship grew very rapidly and movingly. At some point, I became aware that Michael was talking about Sasha as "my son," and in fact he is Sasha's unofficial father, helping him through high school, preparing him for college. He has fed the almost fiendishly intelligent young man volumes of experience and literal volumes on birds and nature. They have been around the world on a floating university and they returned from that voyage by driving across America with more than occasional stops for birds. Michael also calls Sasha "the albatross." He seems to have dedicated his life to him, or at least the few years they can be together, as they travel from birding spot to birding spot, Sasha with his scope ready for the quickest passerine and Michael with his camcorder watching us watching Sasha watching the birds.

Michael is always temperamentally in and of the experience and at the same time almost cynically outside it. The habits of participant-observation fill out the details of his life and it has been difficult to predict either his movements or his momentary interests while we are birding. To this day, a typical Michaelian angularity in his relation to Paul and me and the birds puts an edge on the experience and subtly changes it. On one relatively late date in our birding relationships, Michael, Paul, and I were standing at the edge of a path in some fairly dense woods in Allaire State Park in central New Jersey. It was another one of our May big day migration trips, when together we explore New Jersey, seeking both as many migratory species as we can find and parts of the state we have never seen. These trips—thanks, in particular, to Michael's instinct for exploration—have taught me more about New Jersey than the rest of my twenty-five years here. In the most densely populated state in the country, there are large stretches of wilderness, like McPhee's Pine Barrens (which are not, because of the acidity of the pine-saturated water and the heavy predominance of only a few kinds of trees, good for birds), and areas as remote and rural as parts of the deep South. Allaire itself was not such a place—parts of it were heavily used—but it was for each of us interestingly new; we hadn't sufficient experience to know what bird life we might find there except as William Boyle's precise and inclusive *Guide to Bird Finding in New Jersey* could prepare us. We didn't know what bird it was that had been singing regularly from various spots not far off the path although it was, pretty obviously, some kind of warbler. We had been moving—at least Paul and I had been—with unselfconscious concentration as it flitted erratically alongside the path, just behind the closest of the thickly leaved trees, but after five or ten minutes of guessing which tree it was sitting in and then pursuing it from tree to tree, none of us had managed to spot it.

It was a characteristically tense, frustrating, and delightful moment—three of us intently following with our ears the movements of the bird we could not see, worried that the sound would mute as it does if the bird retreats deeper into the woods, and trying to place it as coming from just there, to the right, and just there, well above eye level, or down there, or over here. We didn't have to worry much about spooking the bird unless we were excessively noisy, since it knew we were there and was moving in the same direction we were. But the art of locating a bird by sound is a very difficult one. Paul has a friend, Richard, who occasionally visits from his home in Mexico and who can in a way that I regard as almost supernatural find just about any bird he hears, track it to its spot in the woods, its particular tree, its very branch. Not so much voyeurism as, maybe, auditeurism? None of us, with our various disabilities of vision and hearing, could do that, although Michael, despite his weak eyes, is pretty good at it. Paul's hearing has faded enough that he usually can't pick up the high-pitched songs of warblers like the blackburnian or the Cape May. So we work very hard for our finds, and this little warbler was proving difficult and elusive.

The frustration of such a moment—having the bird, as it were, almost in one's hand and yet not able to see it—keeps Paul and me jointly focused, working together almost entirely unaware of anything but the bird song and the spaces from which it might be coming. For a while, at least, we act like "natives," not thinking for a second about the participant-observer asking us questions or the camera capturing us. It seemed that Michael was with us in this moment, bound in that ritual quest to see that gives the birding community its purpose, wanting to be able to say, excitedly, "I've got it. There it is." The few times I looked around to see the others, Michael was staying with us in this new territory. This bird interested him, in part, I suspect, because the song was so distinctive yet familiar and, brilliantly clear as it was, so deliciously close, so certainly identifiable, yet so resistant to identification.

As I look back at the moment, similar to many others in different places, I realize that it doesn't matter in the heat of the birding quest who is watching whom or how I might appear—dork, eccentric, naturalist, expert—to anyone else. The energy and the frustration provoked by the evasiveness of the bird can be resolved at last only by seeing it. And Michael did, at last, find it. There. There.

It was one of those climactic moments that focus the pleasures of the birding day, and Michael was not yet withdrawing to anthropological distance. "Hooded," Paul exclaimed. Unfortunately, I lived up to my own sense of myself as birder, for as usual, I was having trouble locating what everyone else was now, at last, comfortably spotting. The bird kept moving, but there was no doubt—the face of the otherwise brilliant yellow warbler is outlined in bold black, reversing the pattern of the common yellowthroat's black mask, but with a boldly marked dark eye. For me, however, struggling to keep up with its darting movements from tree to tree, the actual sighting was a marginal one, and I'm not sure that if Paul and Michael had not told me that the bird was a hooded I would have had a firm enough sighting to claim it. But Michael kept intently watching and listening—as Paul kept trying to lead me to it—and suddenly declared, "The Lone Ranger."

It was an odd, comic, revelatory moment. Michael's call, wonderfully angular again, had transformed the bird's song into the William Tell Overture and, appropriately, the theme music for the Lone Ranger—the masked western hero of our childhoods, who, independent but with his loving sidekick, Tonto, would ride into town to save it and then ride out before anyone could do more than ask of the thankful crowd, "Who was that masked man?" The National Geographic's rendering, "ta-wit ta-wit ta-wit tee-yo," suddenly made sense. Michael's stroke of analogical genius, was, I decided, even superior to his identification of the goldfinch as "potato chip," which makes an interesting if not entirely consistent rendition of the bird's song in flight. Perspective makes analogy possible, and the very distance that Michael's curious relation to us and to birding required seemed to me the condition of his insight, hooking the world of birds to our human conventions. Once we heard the "Lone Ranger" it was unlikely that any of us would ever miss a calling hooded warbler, unless it became perverse enough to vary its song radically.

That theory was put to the test before we were aware of it in the following year when Michael, with his typical intensity, had worked out another itinerary for our spring trip. We were headed far south in New Jersey this time, down toward Dividing River, unfortunately near an atomic power plant but otherwise as remote as one can get in the state. Michael and Paul guessed that this would be prime country for migrating passerines, and partly in the interest of getting off the usual birding routes, a compulsive concern of Michael's, we found ourselves amidst vast areas of private land, entirely unpopulated, with large stands of trees and small gullies everywhere. There certainly were no other birders.

It seemed ripely open space, full of possibilities, precisely the kind of thing that Michael, with his research intensities and need to be both in and away, might find for us. As we surveyed the area from the car and then pulled to a stop, we were wondering what we might find. I pushed open the car door and leaned out. All the self-consciousness, all the watching, all the watching of watchers, all my sensitivity to observing and being observed, all my concern about birding voyeurism, had nothing to do with this moment. There was a call, and before I was fully conscious of what I was hearing I shouted, and thought I heard Paul and Michael shouting simultaneously with a ritual joy of recognition that reaffirmed the unqualified excitement of what we were doing, "The Lone Ranger." The hooded warbler, wherever he was hiding, independent, aloof, but readily identifiable now, was waiting for us on Michael's territory like an old friend with a familiar voice.

white faced ibis?

WHITE-FACED IBIS?

*N*ON-BIRDING acquaintances who hear about any of my birding adventures or catch a name, like yellow-bellied sapsucker or even red-winged blackbird, almost invariably want to know how I know those were the birds in question or how I can trust other people who tell me that the birds were out there somewhere. Can't a bird watcher (non-birders tend to use that phrase) just make up anything? Who is to know? How can an identification be verified? And if you stand up on Hawk Mountain and hear the calls, "rough-legged over two," or "osprey over four," about specks so far away that some people wouldn't even know they were birds, it is hard not to be initially skeptical. I'm not skeptical anymore, not, that is, after the rough-legs and ospreys always turn out to be what they were called.

In the course of my birding travels, I have heard a lot of false calls accepted as true. I have made a lot of false calls, and I'm pretty regularly wrong on whatever it is I say when I first see an unusual bird. Recently, I heard a woman, out to see the aberrant spotted redshank, identify a nearby cormorant as a "great cormorant." Self-evidently, the cormorant was a "double-crested cormorant," and I confirmed that with my friends. But I didn't say a word to the woman or interrupt her rather boastful account of her birding adventures to standers by. What's striking about even such a commonplace story is that I could be so confident about the correct identification.

Of course, there are lots of misidentifications. There is a lot of showing off. There is a lot of puffing and snorting and crudely intruded assertions that show that my list is longer than yours. The egregious birders, usually macho types who would have been better off at football except that it is a contact sport, try to name the bird before you can, contemptuously dismiss any tentativeness in identification, are cruel about errors, and make it clear that they know more and have seen more than you. Such was a fellow named Cy, who barged into our uncompetitive birding set one day at Jones Beach and, after "nailing" half a dozen species with an arrogance that made me wonder what I was doing there, left a trail of hostility behind him. Happily, although Cy was a member of a birding group to which Paul belonged, we have never seen him since. Even more happily, he has proved the exception, rather than the rule.

On the whole, I have been impressed by the birding community. There is a recognizable birding ethos, and one of the joys of birding is that, even in the "Ramble" in Central Park, you can feel comfortable approaching or being approached by someone wearing binoculars and begin a conversation that will be warm, enthusiastic, and in all likelihood helpful. In preparation for a trip out there, I wrote to people in Oregon because they were listed in the ABA directory. One, who was traveling in Alaska when his wife told him about my letter, called from Fairbanks to give me advice about birding spots near Corvallis. He was full of knowledge about places, bird habits, likely sightings, and he was eager to share it with me. He knew, as well, that I would be testing that knowledge, in a way, by going where he recommended, so that the whole relationship entailed a rather high level of trust and honor. I found what he promised me. And when I strike up a conversation with a stranger (wearing binoculars) in the woods, not only am I sure that violence won't follow, but I can tell in just a few sentences whether the information and advice will be reliable, or whether my new acquaintance is a macho lister, or someone struggling, like me, to make sense out of the clues that will allow for a diagnostic identification. Most important, I can always rely on a general understanding of what counts as legitimate identification, of what the standards are.

There are degrees of formality and seriousness in listing. If you want to go public, you had better be very careful. Birders often provide important ornithological data, especially for the various seasonal censuses conducted by major scientific and birding organizations. When the American Ornithological Union accepts an identification, it has been submitted to the most rigorous inquisition. But the kinds of identification I and my friends most often worry about—dependent as they ultimately are on the more rigorously established lists—are for private use. What's to stop us from translating our desires, in the guise of an obscurely seen bird, into a name to make our lists longer? Only, I suppose, that there's not much profit in cheating ourselves. And if we tell our friends about our unlikely spottings, after a while they will stop believing, stop trusting. Each list is a product of the lister's own birding needs, and undoubtedly a lot of cheating does go on, if only the cheating of self-delusion. When I'm ninety-five percent sure that I have seen a bird, I find it extremely difficult not to list it. Sometimes (although I don't tell Paul about that) I do list it.

Identifications among responsible birders are, however, remarkably reliable. When the rare bird alerts announce the presence of a rufous-necked stint, a Eurasian bird wildly off course somewhere in Delaware, you can be sure that such a bird was there, and that if you get to the right place at the right time you will see it. Paul, Michael, Sasha, and I were luckily in that place, and there, among the native sandpipers, was a stunning little bird with a striking rufous head and neck of a kind that simply doesn't exist among American birds. There could be no doubt about it. Whoever first spotted the bird has had the identification confirmed by hundreds, perhaps thousands of birders. Four of us, at least, would be willing to stake our reputations on the validity of the identification.

But of course, I can't speak for the whole birding community. I simply know that when I am out birding in a group, there is a body of knowledge immediately available and a sense of responsibility that accompanies that knowledge so that when someone says, there's a stint, and the sighting is confirmed, a stint is really there: almost nobody cheats, and fewer than that cheat intentionally. Paul and I have been known to fret for long minutes over an unlikely bird until we had every possible field mark. At the end, we ask each other if we are "satisfied," and if either of us is not, the bird flies off unlisted.

Though nobody has seen my life list but me, it is not, finally, an entirely private document. It carries in its names the authority of a community, except where I am willing to be lax and take the risk of cheating myself—which is really relatively infrequently—and even there community knowledge, community standards keep me aware that the listing is not absolutely certain. For ninety-nine percent of the birds on that list, real birds flew into my ken, real feathers, real bills, real colors, real life are represented. Something identifiable was out there in my presence.

And as I take my birding trips, I am eager to extend my claims about avian reality, yes, to make the list longer. Every name implies a rich and complex experience, a confirmation of personal pleasure by the accumulated knowledge of a community of like-minded bird seekers. The AOU may reclassify birds I have seen—so they took away from me the Oregon junco, asserting that it is the same species as the slate-colored junco in my back yard. Now both species are dark-eyed juncos. But the arbitrariness of human classificatory systems on which birding nomenclature is dependent doesn't for a moment diminish the feathery reality of the Oregon juncos I saw in California, whatever we call them now. My naming was reliable then. I've just changed the name. So the list registers something important to me, and each name implies the extension of the experience that must, inevitably, be severely constricted by other responsibilities, by limited powers, and by time.

When I drove out to Utah to teach, I was hoping that I would be getting a whole new Western experience of birds. I needed a change, and Utah, which was both geographically remote and, at the same time, a place with a remarkably interesting English department, seemed a perfect university for me to try. I had seen pictures of the campus with snow-covered mountains surrounding it, and I was told by lots of people, including my son, that it was very beautiful. I was looking for something very beautiful, but I was also hoping that the beauty would include birds. In any case, I was on my own out there, and I brought to the West the ethos of birding I had learned in the East.

There are not a great many species in Utah. It's not really on any of the main flyways, and in my search for the ideal birding book, I found none that treated Utah extensively (although a double issue of the ABA's *Birding* contained some very interesting tips about birding Utah). A high proportion of the species I could see would be new to me and I had a chance of adding substantially to my life list. Real expansion of the list required moving around a lot, getting out of New

Jersey, in particular. The trick would be to find the guides, the time, and the luck. Although my stay in Utah was satisfying in all other respects, I didn't get any of the three. By the time I could go out to do some birding, the hunting season had started, and I wandered through a sanctuary on the Great Salt Lake first wondering why none of the promised ducks was visible and then wondering whether I would survive. The strange popping of shotguns and rifles at first seemed to me an odd acoustic trick until I realized that while I was dying to see the ducks, there were a lot of camouflaged people in blinds, in the brush, all around who were dying to kill them. The ducks were wise, but it took me a little longer.

I escaped with my life and a very short bird list and found myself settling for walks in and around the city, where shooting was less likely, or for trips for fancy/rugged brunches up in the hills on weekends. The mountains were imposing in a way nothing I had experienced in the East could match, and Marge and I drove up into them as far as we could get by car almost every weekend.

On a warm rainy day we drove out of Salt Lake, off the main roads, and suddenly found ourselves in a dangerous snow on a badly rutted and in the end unpaved road, excited and, I confess, scared. We were "saved" by a young man in a pickup truck who, in a Utah-style display of kindness to strangers of a sort that it took me months to get used to, stopped to get out and assure us that the road would get safer, to give us tips about how to maneuver, and provide directions that even a city boy like me couldn't misunderstand. Concentrating on the road, I could barely attend to the two or three hawks, nine or ten thousand feet up but close to our road level, that soared by. But awesomely sublime as the Wasatch mountains were, they were not very birdy. I claimed my life mountain chickadee on a walk near Robert Redford's resort. And at eight thousand feet I saw more than a few Clark's nutcrackers and a gray jay. That was all very nice. And the golden eagle that swooped past the funicular we rode up to Snowbird more than justified the ride. It was not a birdless stay, but I was disappointed, nevertheless, and while I thought my urban anti-hunting thoughts, I was struck by the fact that the hunters with their dogs, their families, and their rifles, looking callously murderous and domestic, knew more about the ducks than I did. I was reminded that they are extremely reliable on bird identifications and that they have a lot more at stake in getting it right than I do. If they're wrong, the wrong bird dies; if they mistake a killdeer for a duck, as George Bush's son did in Texas not long ago, they are subject to severe fines. Birding for them is no abstract or intellectually satisfying pastime, but for the purpose of accurate killing.

Failing with the ducks, I turned to another bird I was particularly eager to see, the Bohemian waxwing. Cedar waxwings, themselves very beautiful with their flattened crests, black masks, smoothly soft brown backs, are fairly common on the East Coast, and I see flocks of them every year. In the hill just above our house in Salt Lake there were trees full of cedar waxwings. But I have never seen a Bohemian. Hoping for a sighting of this slightly larger bird with white and yellow markings on its wings, and with what was surely hubris, I had bought a startlingly attractive and bold art photograph of Bohemians feeding on berries in the snow. But the year passed without a Bohemian waxwing and without anyone to take me to where one might be. I have been told that I should only buy pictures of the birds after I have seen them, as I did with the prothonotary. I will hold to that rule from now on.

There was, however, one interesting trip that ended by not increasing my life list and by putting birding honor to the test. Late in the fall, when I thought I had found a place relatively safe from hunters, I persuaded Marge to join me for a ride that was sure to be visually interesting, and she agreed that we would stop for just a little birding at Farmington Bay, where migrating birds are reputed to stage in abundance. But it was late in the season and I wasn't optimistic. The area was flat, scenically undramatic, or dramatic only as the almost moonscape quality of the Great Salt Lake area can be.

The migration was just about over. I had heard that there were hundreds of phalarope to be seen, but by the time I got there I could find only one, a Wilson's, in non-breeding plumage. The Wilson's is striking in breeding plumage, with a sweep of rust extending down the upper breast from its beginnings in a black eye patch, but in the plumage I was seeing it was an undistinguished shore-bird brown and dirty white; only its long needlelike bill made it stand out among the other stragglers. There was not a lot else to see. In my latest disappointment, as I was about to suggest to Marge that we return to the car, I saw just to the side of the water an imposing, long-legged wading bird with a steeply curved bill, darkly walking across the path. It paused, I had what I thought was a good look, and I immediately said to myself with some disappointment, "glossy ibis." Not that I don't love to see glossy ibises, but that I see them all the time through the spring and summer in appropriate places on the East Coast. This was a very familiar bird and I turned away and not long after drove off with Marge.

The problem came later when, with my bird literature assembled, I discovered that what I had seen was probably a white-faced ibis, not a glossy. What was a clumsy birder to do? The bird I had seen answered almost perfectly the description of the glossy, but I was insufficiently careful and curious. Glossys don't turn up in Utah while white-faced summer there, and then in the autumn migrate south to Texas and Mexico. The bird simply had to have been a white-faced ibis, but I didn't know it when I saw it. Question: do I list this lifebird or not?

If you're a birder of my type, it is difficult not to be aware of the potential silliness of "listing." The American Birding Association, full though it is of first-class birders and ornithologists, is a listing association. Every year it publishes its list of listers. So in a supplemental number of its journal, it is possible to find which of its members has seen the most birds in the world, the most birds in the United States, the most birds in a particular state. There are endless refinements to listing.

While I keep only a U.S. list, it is not unusual to find birders who keep lists for every country and state they visit. There are also backyard bird lists, although they don't make the ABA publication. There are annual lists (I do keep one for myself) noting how many species people have seen during the past year. As an indication of the limits of my birding life, it might be worth revealing that I have never seen more than 234 species in any given year. My total U.S. list is now hovering around four hundred species. All the more reason why a successful stay in Utah was such an attractive possibility for me. And all the more reason why I am still kicking myself for not having been prepared for the white-faced ibis.

The questions about validity of identification are, of course, crucial for listers. For if one is going to list, one must make some rules about what constitutes fair listing. Absurd as it may seem, such rules are indispensable, even for the unofficial birder whose list is entirely private. Here are some of the tricky birders' questions: Do you list birds only heard not seen? Do you accept an identification of a bird you have only glimpsed but everybody else has firmly identified? Do you list birds found dead? Do you list birds that have escaped from their cages and are living in the wild? Even Paul, who doesn't care how long his list is, has had to develop listing rules. He does keep records of what he sees—not to show off to other birders but as one might want to keep a diary, a vital reminder of one's activities in the past. For me as for most birders, first sightings often have a vividness that recurs with each new sighting and that rises off the dullest bird ledger, even the Linnaean Society field card that provides spaces for checking off every bird likely to be seen in the Northeast. For Paul, accepting a lifebird is a pretty serious business. And his rule is, "If you wouldn't eat it, don't claim it."

The rule is built on an analogy with mushrooms. One must treat the identification of birds as though making the claim would have life or death consequences—the same consequences as if you mistook a poisonous mushroom for an edible one. It is a wonderfully reasonable rule, and it is designed, very effectively, to keep you honest. I don't know whether other birders are as rigorous as Paul in this respect. But there is no point fooling oneself or allowing one's desire to determine what's out there. We can talk about "probables"—that was *probably* an alder flycatcher, for example—but one can't list them, either as lifebirds or as trip birds.

Paul's standards are even higher than that. Given that one shouldn't claim a bird about which there is any doubt at all, he goes on to say that one shouldn't claim a lifebird unless one has oneself seen all that one needs to see to make an identification—unless, to revert to Peterson, the field marks have been, to your own eye, diagnostic. And beyond that—although this is a rule to which we are all only partially faithful—one shouldn't claim a bird by way of negation, by virtue, that is, of the question, "What else could it be?" Very often, it is possible to see birds that don't offer "diagnostic" features but that seem to belong in the place, and that have no subtly differentiated counterparts who might have slipped in accidentally.

All of these rules seem pretty comfortable out there in the field. The very rigorousness with which, in his quiet way, Paul adheres to the highest standards of birding integrity make it obvious that he is not in it for the competition. I have never found out from Paul precisely how extensive his bird lists are. I have, on the other hand, found him deriving the most exquisite pleasure from just one more extended sighting of birds he has seen hundreds of times, of, say, a harlequin duck, or of a Blackburnian warbler with its throat of less than an inch of flaming orange—"firethroat," he calls it.

Often, in the silence of my post-field deliberations, I find it difficult to adhere to Paul's rules. What difference would it make if I said what I am sure is true, that the bird was a white-faced ibis? Could I in fact say it and yet not list it because the conditions of the sighting were wrong? I *saw* a glossy ibis, but it was a white-faced ibis.

The questions sometimes remind me of medieval scholasticism, but in my birding mode they are serious and give me some idea of why metaphysics seemed so important for so many Western millennia. Subtle refinements and discriminations become essential. The ABA, for example, doesn't allow the listing of escapes. If a parrot gets out of its New York apartment and sets up house in Central Park (as has happened), no respectable ABA member could list that parrot as a lifebird or tripbird or New York bird. (But how can one know, Borges might have asked, that the wild parrot is the same as the one that escaped?) If the parrot survives and mates and produces little parrots, after some specified number of bird generations its heirs become legitimate for listing.

Once, in one of the more exciting moments of my birding life, I took a detour through our local park to cool down from a difficult day's work, when I spotted an odd-looking duck on the pond. I stared as determinedly as I could and couldn't match what I saw with any American duck I knew about. So I ran home for my binoculars and my field guide, ran back to the pond, and there it was again. But even with binoculars it gave me no American clue. So I ran back for my British field guide and for Marge, on whom I constantly inflict these spasms of birding excitement, and as the bird sat contentedly on the pond, clearly there for a long time, I checked the British guide, and sure enough, it was a ruddy shelduck. After watching it for a long time and confirming over and over again this identification, I went home to call the Audubon Society to announce my discovery and ask if they wanted to investigate themselves. I really did have fantasies of widespread birding fame as I would be announced as the discoverer of this European duck in New Jersey waters.

The society official was not moved and did not offer to make me famous. He told me that there had been other sightings of the shelduck, as far north as Boston, and that what undoubtedly had happened is that some shelducks brought to Cape May for study had escaped. This was not a bird, it was an escape. I never got to enter the ruddy shelduck on my American life list although the memory of it sitting on a pond in Highland Park is as vivid as if it had been listable.

Or what if the bird you see happens to be dead? On the beach this summer I noted a dark, gull-sized bird sitting alone in the sand, too weak to attempt to escape the many passing joggers and strollers. I stopped two curious children from touching it, but I couldn't remain there and it was evident that it hadn't long to live, whether or not humans hastened it on its way out. Sensing death, I was thrilled to see that this was no gull at all but a pelagic bird, one that normally spends its life far enough out to sea that it would never make itself known even to beach dwellers. The tubular nose and general configuration led me to recognize that the gull-like appearance was deceptive and that this was in fact a "tubenose," one of a large family of ocean birds that includes such exotic creatures as the albatross, as well as fulmars, shearwaters, and petrels. This bird, sitting within three feet of me, was surely a greater shearwater.

It was as close as I will ever get to one of those pelagic creatures, which I romanticize regularly in part because I am such a poor sailor. It was close enough to guarantee identification. I could stand beside it with my field guide open and check every field mark. The bird was going nowhere, but I wasn't cheating. Yet I couldn't reconcile the pleasure I was taking in seeing it so precisely with the knowledge that I could only see it because it was dying. In a fit of conscience, I raced to the house and called everyone I could who might help rescue the bird, but there was nobody available who could get here before the tide turned. And so, as the bird lay dying, I confirmed the sighting with my other bird books. No doubt about it, a real greater shearwater was sitting a few feet away from me on the beach at Biddeford Pool. If I had come a few hours later, had the tide not swept it away, it would have been dead. There was no rule, however, against listing a dying bird. Since it was still alive, I could list it. And I did.

But the white-faced ibis, very much alive, is not listed. It might take another trip to Utah for me to identify one confidently. Birding honor requires of me that I not list it because, in certain crucial metaphysical ways, I never saw it. It is even remotely possible, since such things do happen, that it was a glossy ibis blown way off course. After all, a rufous-necked stint turned up in Delaware.

I know what a white-faced ibis looks like from the bird books, not from that experience out at Farmington Bay. I'm not absolutely sure to this moment whether I would "eat it," although I am ready to take that chance. Wrestling with the problem, I knew that Paul would not give me any help but would leave it to my conscience to make the decision, and I was right. "You didn't expect me to help you decide, did you?" he e-mailed back to me, after I posed the question. No, I guess not. But as my birding conscience, he did in fact decide for me. I knew that under the same circumstances, he wouldn't have listed it.

So I ended by trusting myself on questions of identification, and trusting myself, I realized, meant that I trusted the birding ethos that by and large governs the casual, mistake-prone, bird-loving community of amateurs and ornithologists who call out "rufous-necked stint," "spotted redshank," "double-crested cormorant." Those calls have led to some of the most satisfying moments of my life.

chimney swift

SWIFTS

$\mathcal{A}$ ARON CALLS ME "Zaydee," to distinguish me from his grandfather on my son-in-law's side, who is "Pop-Pop." I was at first a little disoriented by the name, for I remember it only as a term used to describe my father's father, a gentle old man whom I did not know well and who was very religious. I am neither religious, nor gentle as he was. But Zaydee I am, and I'm getting to like it. Especially because it comes in the voice of Aaron.

For the most part, I have had to keep birding and family apart, except as I have implied connections in the course of these narratives. Aaron may be changing that, or it may be that I am hoping I can use him to change that. I fear I know the birds better than I know my family, and I want to know them together. As Aaron grows, I am waiting for him to take up the succession created and then broken by my son and now, at two-and-a-half years old, he may be ready. My daughter, Rachel, has been indoctrinating him, perhaps to indulge my eccentricity. For whatever reason, Aaron is fascinated by owls, particularly by the owl figures set up at the New Brunswick, New Jersey, railroad station. Now there's an owl at Edison, which is closer to where he lives, and he regularly reports to me, and anyone who will listen, that there's an owl in New Brunswick. Yesterday, he called to tell me that there's an owl at Edison.

All of this cutesy stuff, which might just a few years ago have seemed beyond the pale of my taste and imagination, now moves me, as I suppose it moves most grandparents who find in their first grandchild miracles of cleverness and beauty. Aaron, like the rest of the family, is getting woven into my imagination of birds, and I would like to do it better this time. Not that the whole family has not for the most part indulged me in the bird obsession that took possession of me some twenty years ago. But there is in that indulgence a kind of smiling condescension, a recognition that the old guy has his oddities, and this is a relatively pleasant one. So, when a particularly birdy nature show is on television, I often receive a call from Rachel telling me to watch Channel 13. When I visit New Mexico, David arranges for a trip to nearby bird sanctuaries. If this is an eccentric's indulgence, I'm ready to be an eccentric now and wish I had known how to be one when I was younger. It's a way for us all to connect around the evasions and indirections that characterize so much of the emotional life of so many families. I'll take it.

In my spare time I plot how to seduce Aaron into really wanting to know about birds. Too heavy a hand too early would be fatal, although Michael, who has been very successful with children of friends and who, with Sasha, has created something of a birding monster, thinks I should come down with a heavy hand, or talon, and make Aaron aware at every moment of the presence and the fascination of birds. So far, I haven't bought him any bird books, although he reads everything in sight. He is as yet far better at classifying railroad freight cars than birds. I think about taking him for a walk in the local woods, but I can't imagine getting him to focus for so long, and he's obviously not ready for binoculars yet.

The best I have been able to do is what Rachel does. As we walk through the streets and birds attract our attention (or even if they don't quite), I name them. There's a pigeon. There's a robin. Since everything seems to sink into that brain, an instrument that my watching Aaron grow has evoked from me much increased respect, and since he will often speak back to us days later information that we thought he had ignored, I am hoping the discriminations will be happening. Certainly, he learned something about owls, or wooden owls, in Cold Spring, New York.

In the window of one of the antique stores, Aaron saw a carving of a large owl. He was fascinated by it, and every time we entered the town, he would ask to see the owl. We talked about it a lot, and then we noticed, in a store just a few windows down, another owl. I pointed it out to Aaron. It was a very different-looking creature, much smaller, without the characteristic shape of the imposing great horned owl, thinner, leaning a bit to the side. Aaron was just a little puzzled by this other kind of owl. That, I said to Aaron, is a screech owl. The one in the other window is a great horned owl. He said nothing in response, and seemed not to care much about the smaller bird.

We got a report a few days later from Rachel that on their next visit to town, Aaron took her to the windows. He pointed out "the great horned owl," and then wanted to show them the "screech owl." It was a day of triumph for me—an ornithologist may be in the making. I wondered if he also remembered who gave him that information in the first place. At least, through what may well be normal infantile curiosity and absorptiveness, although it seems prodigal to the grandfather, Aaron may be offering me a chance for my second important family birding connection.

I think a lot about chances missed. Each of Paul's children is now working in some aspect of conservation, biology, or ecology. They didn't start out that way. There were the usual family tensions among them, and the boy, like his father before him, became a ski bum for a while. (Paul says that his son was much better at it than he was.) One of the daughters rebelled fiercely for a while, though the rebellion had nothing to do with birds, later became a lawyer for an ecological outfit, and seems now to have settled down into full-time motherhood. Another of the daughters is a serious biologist, has traveled all over the world, but focuses her research on local matters. Their mother had divorced Paul, not simply, of course, over birds. (In fact, Paul tells me, while she was ambivalent about birding when they were married, birding is perhaps the biggest topic of conversation they still share, aside, of course, from the pleasure they take in the way their children and grandchildren seem to be turning out.) But he always spent a lot of time camping with the kids or taking them on nature trips, and my son David was introduced to birding by Paul's son, Peter. For one year in England, he went out regularly with Paul and Peter and his sister Gretchen on apparently very satisfying and interesting birding trips. I remember in particular their exuberant report on an astoundingly rich visit to the sanctuary at Minsmere in David Copperfield country, where I did not go, never thought about going.

On David's twelfth birthday, I did drive him and Paul and Peter to Wales, not for my natural literary objectives, Tintern Abbey or Mount Snowden, but for the birds. And I remember sitting in the woods quietly as they studied the movements of a variety of tits, although I wasn't sufficiently interested to learn which ones, and always had a dirty little infantile pun on my mind. Once I slammed to a stop when someone screamed "green woodpecker." That's about all I can remember of those birds. I was interested in David's pleasure, but not in what David was interested in.

And I think how much richer an early relationship we might have developed if we had gone camping, as Paul and his family often happily did, even though since my boy scout days and army bivouacking I have done what I could to avoid camping. I was thinking about my professional life, and birds and camping were uncomfortable intrusions on it. Wales was an important place on my literary, not my ornithological map. And when with the family we visited Wales on another occasion, I was most interested in the now famous little town of Hay-on-Wye, which has more books and bookstores per capita than any place in the world. It was at Hay-on-Wye that I bought my luscious, expensive, beautiful Cook and Wedderburn edition of John Ruskin's works, an indulgence that I am still enormously pleased to have given myself. Not thinking of Ruskin's own love of birds and nature, I was in love with the wonderful paper and illustrations and annotations of that still much sought-after edition of his works.

It is of course a fantasy to think of that other kind of relationship with David that I never had; I was not the person to have that relationship. I wasn't even aware of it as an absence. David was a beautiful boy who was easy to travel with, and we took him to the Tower of London and to Stonehenge, where we photographed him and Rachel standing between the stones, and he sat on the red lion outside the Red Lion Inn in Salisbury, and we even took him and Rachel to meet our friends in Venice, where the only birds we thought about were the ubiquitous pigeons. (Rock doves I call them now, when I am listing.) Certainly that was okay.

But the birds weren't there to connect us, and I often now think enviously of relations Paul must have had with his kids on those outings and camping trips. I haven't told Paul of that envy or asked him what really happened, how much the kids enjoyed it, how much he did, whether relationships tightened within earshot of lifebirds and in front of a fire. But whatever happened then, somehow Paul's children have all come through their rebellions and resistances and curved back to his own passions for nature, making their lives out of work that he and I value greatly.

Ironically, my kids, resistant to me and my books and my literary commitments, have also curved back to me, although I imagine—probably inaccurately—that Paul never felt that he had lost touch along the way, while I know, from the intimacies of our day-to-day life, that I did. The curve, in this case, includes something of my own skepticism of avocations like birding. But I am pleased after all that David and Rachel, willy nilly, love books and have gone into the arts, and Aaron is the next generation heir of that literary commitment. I can say with some comfort and only a touch of sentimentality that I feel pride in their work and their decisions, and am at the same time bemused to find that I have come out somewhere else than where they have gone in their curving back.

I sometimes fantasize that I could start again, and make it better and easier for everyone. Professionally, I dream, I would make myself an ornithologist. And then I remember that my brother started that way in fact. His theory now is that the ideal dreams of childhood—to become a dancer, a pianist, a sports star, a birder, an actress—all must be outgrown. Reality sets in, and those fantasies, like his own collegiate imagination of being a wildlife conservationist, must be put aside. He is suspicious of David, who insists on writing. He is suspicious of Rachel, who has stayed in the theater, although he is pleased to hear how very seriously she takes her work, how very hard she drives herself at it. Staying with dreams is usually a form of laziness.

I dream that I could have stayed with dreams, or had them. The dreams now tend to get focused on the birds. I dreamed of being a writer. I dream now of taking Aaron out into the woods, of showing him some of their marvels, of being there when he first spots the scarlet of the scarlet tanager, the orange and black of the oriole, the hovering of the kestrel, or sees for the first time in the wild the owls that now so richly fill his imagination. I would love to take him to see and hear the cranes, to listen to the booming of the prairie chicken, and I would love to have him show me birds I have never seen before, lifebirds.

At the moment, Aaron is in love with wheels, and birds, alas, have wings. Railroads and automobiles and bicycles and windmills and all things that spin are his passion. I hope, however, that birds will matter to him. Not only the duck telephone in my kitchen, or the owl at the New Brunswick railroad station, but those things really flying around out there. Of course, although I hope there are as many species around when he is an adult as there were when I started birding, that again is likely to be fantasy. Still, I hope they link him, as they have linked me, lovingly to a world from which it is almost impossible not to feel alienated and against which his Uncle David lives his life and writes his narratives.

I hope he remembers, as happily as I do and will, the summer evening we were walking down the street of Cold Spring toward the railroad station, where he delighted in the passing "Metro North" or "Amtrak," which he was quick to identify, and in remembering the conductor's handing him a sheaf of tickets for punching. As we strolled, hand in hand, he noticed a bird on the pavement. "That's a sparrow, Zaydee," he said. We were birding. And I pushed it.

Overhead there was the twittering of chimney swifts, a characteristic and for me bracing sound of early summer evenings. Swifts dart and sweep across the sky seemingly unbalanced and with uneven wingbeats, but the books all say that's an illusion. It doesn't matter: they have an unmistakable flight, make unmistakable non-musical twittering sounds, fundamentally distinct from the sound of swallows. Their shape is utterly simple. Peterson, wonderfully, describes it as "a cigar with wings," sickle-shaped wings, as I see them.

All this, I realized, was not going to register with Aaron, but

I looked up, and pointed there for him to see. I don't know whether he did in fact see them, but he surely knew what I was talking about when I told him, "Those birds are swifts." Here was one more possible species for his life list. He thought seriously, looking up at where the swifts were darting. "Actually, Zaydee," he said with mature seriousness, "they call them sea gulls."

I have no idea where that came from, and you can be sure that some day I will test him on "sea gulls," and even perhaps bully him into acknowledging that there is no such thing as a "sea gull." Each of those gulls has a specific name—herring gull, black-backed gull, Bonaparte's gull, ring-billed gull, laughing gull. But that's for later. Now, I indulged the absurd cuteness of the moment with grandfatherly amusement. I didn't argue. At least Aaron had worked through to a category, "birds," and in that category, both swifts and sea gulls do have a place. No doubt there are refinements to be made, and I'm hoping that I can make them with him.

Being the eccentric grandfather is okay. I will use that eccentricity to make Aaron laugh and to find excuses to be with him alone on increasingly lengthy birding excursions. It's a chance at another beginning and at other linkages. No doubt he won't remember that moment, and if it were recalled to him he might be embarrassed. I can narrate it only with irony at my own expense, at the degree to which I have outside of narrative allowed myself to become the parody of the doting grandfather. But even the irony is qualified by the seriousness of my ambition: there's no connection between gulls and swifts that I can think of and I will try some day to teach Aaron the difference.

greater shearwater

KITTIWAKE

OCEAN VOYAGES have not been pleasant for me. My first serious one was on a troopship from New York to Bremerhaven. We slept in a hold, four tiers of cots, ripe smells, widespread discontent. I was on the third tier, and two rows over, on the first tier, there was a soldier who peed in his sleep. Each day we would be regularly herded on deck so that the hold could be cleaned out, and the seas seemed always to be rough as we swayed in crowds and waited for permission to go below. It was thirteen days to Bremerhaven on the USS *General Blatchford*, and I was saved—at least psychologically—by a soldier who had been an English major in college. Fresh with an MA, I was full of stuff that nobody in that hold would have begun to care about, but for hours the English major and I would argue about Marxism and literature, whether Shakespeare could be any good if he were politically retrograde. And if he were any good, what did that do to a theory that required of literature a progressive political orientation or influence. It's hard to imagine that I was really talking that way under those circumstances and in that place. Vaguely, although I can't remember the English major's name, I can recollect invoking *Richard II* as evidence against the crude Marxism that I was finding in fact quite seductive and to which I was responding with what I am sure was equally crude aestheticism. We ignored constant demands that we shut up, and as I have thought about it over the years I have wondered at how lightly the other wretched members of that hold let us off. If I had been forced to listen to that sophomoric talk for thirteen days, I would have been shouting shut up, too. But we hung on to literature as a way to dispel the nightmare of the voyage. Nothing about the sea looked attractive to me. Its enormous turbulent emptiness was new and frightening, and I certainly was not on the lookout for pelagic birds. I had never heard of pelagic birds except for Coleridge's albatross, and even with an MA, I didn't now the word pelagic, anyway.

Not quite so wretched in my memory was a forced voyage on the old *Queen Mary*. Marge, Rachel, David, and I were spending a year in London, and when it came time to return, an airline strike canceled our flight. There was no clue as to when the strike would end; our plans were in place; we had to go. After shopping around desperately for a way back to America, work, and home, I at last had to call my father for assistance: the only booking possible was second class on the *Queen Mary*, a far more luxurious trip than we could afford. With some help, however, we booked and I was slightly relieved to know that the trip was guaranteed not to take more than five days. Five days are certainly better than thirteen, but when they came, those days, too, were rough ones. While steel-stomach Rachel—three-and-a-half and hungry—forced Marge to take her down for dinner each day, where they dined in lonely abundance, David and I were virtually passed out from powerful seasick pills dispensed by the ship nurse. I have an obscure memory of rousing myself when Marge and Rachel returned to the cabin one day, agreeing that I needed some food and accepting an apple; but I never ate it, for I quickly faded from consciousness again.

One problem with being prone to seasickness is that you are not likely to see a significant portion of the world's bird population, much of which lives almost entirely at sea and nests on rocky islands inaccessible to normal human traffic. That greater shearwater I saw on the beach at Biddeford Pool, waiting to die or for the tide to sweep it out again, is the kind of bird you almost certainly won't see from land unless it is dying and caught by the tides to be swept up on a beach loaded with humans. That is one of the reasons that birders love hurricanes.

In hurricanes, anything can happen: birds get blown violently off course so that species you would never expect might be sitting on somebody's lawn or roof or telephone line. Perhaps, in such storms, you can see pelagic birds while you scan from the beach, that is, if you can withstand the elements. I saw my first peregrine falcon in the wake of a hurricane. Wade, my ornithologist friend, who, in his ornithological authority, had some compassion for poor amateurs like me, suggested to Michael, who in turn suggested to me, that the day a hurricane was supposed to hit the Jersey shore we should go out birding. I thought they were both mad and Michael yet more so, but learned that this is the way of the serious birder; and so I ventured out. The hurricane glanced off the vulnerable Jersey shore and did only minor damage so that by the time we got to the shore, the sun was shining, the wind was way down, and Wade was rather disappointed. The surf may have been the most impressive I have ever seen, there was debris everywhere, and right by the beach, on some telephone wires that had survived, sat a peregrine falcon. I began to see the virtues of hurricanes.

Nevertheless, catastrophe is not an essential component of

every sighting of pelagic birds from the land. Good and experienced birders have impressive lists of alcids (or "auks," penguin-like diving seabirds), petrels, shearwaters, gannets, kittiwakes. "Watch for them from coastal points during nasty weather," suggests Peterson about the alcids. Even I have seen some, and when the sun was shining. Out on the coast of Oregon, at the Yaquina lighthouse, there are easily visible colonies of common murres and pigeon guillemots, both alcids. Out of Jonesport, Maine, Captain Barna Norton will take you in his fishing boat to Machias Seal Island, which he claims for the USA but which officially belongs to Canada. On that island, after you step, very gingerly, through a field of nesting arctic terns that will bombard you and peck pretty seriously at your head to protect their chicks, you will find a huge colony of puffins and razorbills. Given its shortness, I didn't hesitate to make that trip, which provided me with my best closeup look at puffins and my "life" razorbill. Birders at Montauk Point, even in my presence, often claim to see alcids. A razorbill or two invariably zips by while I am watching the scoters, and though I never see them I believe they have been there. I do regularly see gannets, beautiful white (with a touch of rufous on the head) tapered gull-like birds with pointed wings that facilitate their remarkable fishing dives from great heights.

Sighting seabirds from land has its excitement, of course, but it doesn't capture the sense of the bird at sea, nor do I want to wait vampirishly until they all sicken like the greater shearwater and crawl onto the beach to die for me to see them. The list of pelagic birds I haven't seen is embarrassingly long.

If my passion for birds were as intense as I pretend, I would do something about that. I think of Charles Darwin, whose writings have come to fascinate me professionally and personally and about whom I have published a good deal. Darwin fell in love with the tropics by way of Humboldt's travel narratives, and when the opportunity for a voyage to the tropics and around the world came up, he took it immediately—with the support, of course, of his uncle and his very wealthy father. The fact that Darwin was a terrible sailor was no impediment. Many admire him for his intellectual achievements, for his world-transforming formulation of an evolutionary hypothesis and of his later confirmed theory of natural selection. I admire him yet more for his very British willingness to remain at sea when every day was a physical misery. After five years, he never got used to the motion of the waters. And during all that time, cramped in a cabin not very much larger than a closet, rooming with an irascible sea captain, he kept at his work. Where would the theory of evolution be had Darwin let seasickness get him down? And where are my alcids and petrels and shearwaters, all the pelagics that live outside my earthen world? Beyond my reach because I can't bear the memory of thirteen days to Bremerhaven.

I have tried to be brave, especially since my passion for birds and my love of Darwin have intensified my fascination with a natural world that I continue to regard as unimaginably beautiful and persistently hostile. I have dabbled in the ocean on tourist whale trips during our annual summers in Maine—four- to eight-hour excursions out into deeper waters in order to watch the whales breach and dive. Whales may be as beautiful as birds, but they're big and they're mammals and they don't fly. Nevertheless, they make a superb and yet comfortable excuse for pelagic birding, an excuse so seductive that Marge is happy to join me—as long as we both are loaded with dramamine. Prepared for one such trip, we dosed ourselves heavily at seven in the morning, drove to the ship and found that weather had canceled the tour. We could barely walk back to the car and I don't know how we managed to drive back to our summer rental, where we collapsed into bed and slept through the day.

We tried it again, however, in the next week, and this time

with success. While most of the passengers were gathered to watch the whales, I placed myself strategically for a glimpse at the pelagic birds. Happily, the captain was sensitive to other forms of life than whales, and he called our attention to bald eagles and osprey nesting on islands close in shore. I didn't need his help to notice those wonderful red-legged black guillemots, alcids that tend in breeding time to stay close to shore on the East Coast as the pigeon guillemot stays close to shore on the West Coast. I was eager to see not only alcids— particularly those that won't come in close to shore—but petrels and shearwaters, gannets and kittiwakes. On this whaling trip, we saw a lot of whales and that was sufficient to satisfy everyone, even me.

But the most stunning moment of the trip came when, as we reached the farthest point from land, we glided by an extraordinarily flat, glassy, calm patch of water, rather like a pond in the middle of the ocean. The captain stopped the ship and we swayed gently in the surrounding currents, currents that seemed not to affect the glassy patch, which, in the midst of vast stretches of choppy emptiness, attracted flocks of sea birds—dozens, perhaps hundreds of petrels and shearwaters skimmed the reflecting surface. They were feasting on fish that all but leaped to their mouths as their feet dabbled in the water and they seemed to be strolling through an improbable and very wet garden.

The mysteriously placid and edenic place was almost more fascinating to me than the birds, which were the first petrels and shearwaters I had ever seen. Everything was domestic scale. The petrels were small birds, surprisingly small I thought, having had no experience of them. Storm petrels, which the book notes as being much smaller than the "gadfly" petrels that dwell at great distances from Maine and the northeast coast, are barely as big as robins. When they flash by a ship, they are usually mere dark spots to the untrained eye.

For this landlubber it was an almost miraculous sight, as

though there really were a garden out there and the flowers were all in bloom bringing to it the inevitable finches and robins and hummingbirds. But these were no domesticated birds, not birds to expect at the feeder. I had heard of storm petrels but really had no idea what they looked like. They seemed far beyond the possibilities of my experience, like the worlds of eighteenth-century gothic romances. I imagined them having vague romantic associations, dwelling mystically in the mind of some sturm-und-drang German composer, or haunting the remote geographic margins of narratives like *Frankenstein* or Coleridge's famous "Rime." Most striking and moving about what I was watching was that while all the "pattering, hopping motions" of these comfortably feeding birds were taking place beyond sight of land in vast spaces that constitute the worlds of nightmare or vision, the texture of the place and of the birds that occupied it was very much like that of an English garden. The Wilson's storm petrels skittered along the surface, hopping like robins, or like white-throated sparrows scratching the leaves away for seeds. They were small and manageable birds, no more majestic than, say, barn swallows. This is not to diminish them or minimize the loveliness of their stark blacks and whites (all storm petrels are black and white). The domesticity in the midst of so much that was potentially threatening, and coming as part of a quest to see the largest mammals in the world, was pleasantly disorienting. I had no idea such places existed, and the captain's quite mundane explanation of why the water in that small area remained so smooth or why there were so many fish for bird dinner did not correspond to the moment and the vision. Nor could it, of course, compete with the elation I was feeling at having found in one place at one time four lifebirds.

Identifying what I was seeing was not so easy. I found the petrels as hard to discriminate as I find the "peeps," those little six-inch sandpipers that run like windup toys along the tidal edges. I was prepared for birding excitement, but not for the difficulties of birding subtleties. I had to work hard: the distinctions are minute and require time and training, as well as some pretty severe disciplining of desire. Happily, the boat was stopped and the birds were pleased enough with the fishing not to be going anywhere. With some stress, anxiety, and fear that I wouldn't really "eat" the calls, I think I figured out Wilson's and Leach's storm petrels, primarily on the strength of the size and shape of the rump bands. This would have been an impossible discrimination if the birds had been simply passing, and even now I'm not sure that my identifications are up to the standards Paul would be using. I thought I caught a difference in tail shape also: the Leach's has a forked tail while Wilson's is basically flat. Retrospectively, especially since I have not seen either of those birds since, I don't feel entirely comfortable with the identifications, but out there on the sea, with plenty of time and lots of birds, the distinctions seemed clear. The shearwaters were naked-eye different from the petrels, but perhaps even less different from each other. They required yet more anxiety and hard work, more doubt. In the end I was willing to acknowledge both the Cory's and the greater, the latter perhaps an ancestor of the bird I found on the beach in Biddeford Pool. I needed a true birder along, someone patient enough to talk me through the subtleties of the markings and the shapes and the movements, but I was the most accomplished birder on the ship. Naming, which is so much a part of the birder's experience, so much the way in which to make some sense of minuscule and massive differences and entanglements of nature, was only part of the pleasure, and the lesser part for that moment. The primary part was the vision of the ocean garden and the vitality of that little world of fish and birds in the midst of the vast blankness of the sea.

One whaling trip does not a birder make; my pelagic list remained painfully small. But with the first good experience of my ocean-going career behind me, I suggested to Paul that perhaps we might try one of the regular pelagic birding trips sponsored by groups like New Jersey Audubon or the Cape May Bird Observatory. And he—rather a good sailor to begin with—agreed. In order to reduce the chances that we would run into the violence of winter storms, I pointed toward the latest possible date on which the birds might be there. Of course I was nervous about it, but after all I had my parallel to Darwin's imagination of the tropics and I would risk discomfort for the chance at alcids and kittiwakes and gannets.

It was chilly that morning and although it was still dark as we stepped on board the ship, there were signs that the sky was densely clouded. As we pulled away from the dock and I knew that for at least eight hours my comfort would be determined by the whims of the sea, I was almost sure I had made a mistake. But I could barely admit it to myself and certainly not to Paul or anyone else on the boat. I hadn't counted on the degree of discomfort. As the light began to ooze through the clouds it was evident that we were in for trouble. The feeble dawn light did not strengthen as we eased into what should have been day but that turned out to be a gray rain. Although I was partly doped up from dramamine, I was too anxious to feel really tired. At first, my primary concern was to keep my binoculars dry enough so that if a bird did appear, I would be able to see it.

It finally brightened enough through the rain and the increasingly rough sea that we could see pretty clearly several hundred yards on all sides of us. As we dipped and rose with increasing irregularity, not much appeared. There were occasional signs of bird life, darkly speeding by, but I couldn't get beyond agreeing that they were birds. My glasses were not only wet on the outside, but moisture was somehow getting in them. The birder's worst nightmare was coming true: my glasses were fogging in such a way that I could not wipe them dry. Gradually, as I raised them to my eyes to catch some fleeting image, things faded into foggy obscurity, and as the ship tossed with increasing violence, I began to lose my energy for seeing anything. The chill cut in under my raingear. There was wetness everywhere. Nausea began to take me and I had a sense that the dramamine was wearing off. I struggled below, losing sight of my primary reason for being there—to see the pelagic birds who apparently liked this sort of weather—and chilled, wet, nauseated, I sought the bag in which I kept the supplementary dramamine. Tough birders were hauling themselves to the railings, throwing up over the side, and raising their binoculars, when they were functioning, to see if anything might be out there. Glasses defunct, stomach virtually so, I could only hope that a second dramamine would keep me stable enough until we got back to land. I took the luxury of surrendering to my misery as my thoughts turned entirely to the question of how much longer this could go on.

I did find a pill but had nothing to down it with. I tried swallowing it dry and began gagging. Nothing could go down. Everything wanted to come up. I tossed the pills away and struggled to find a place out of the worst of the weather, where I could sit and shiver and wait for shore. I hadn't the heroic stamina of many of the birders on the boat (nor a pair of working binoculars). When a very occasional call of "petrel at two o'clock" reached me huddled on a bench and shivering, I didn't look up. Paul's glasses finally fogged too. My hope then was that the captain would not hold to the eight-hour schedule, that given the rough seas and the low visibility and the steady rain, he would turn around and get us home as soon as possible. I certainly wasn't going to ask for a refund. In fact, three hours into the cruise, he did turn us around, which meant to my rapidly calculating mind that the trip might last only six hours instead of eight.

I suppose that the misery was not absolute. Trailing in the boat's wake there was a cluster of gulls, to which Paul was entirely alert. "Kittiwake," he called encouragingly. In other circumstances, it would have been a moment of exuberance.

Here, it managed to give some meaning to five hours of extreme discomfort. As I remember it, I saw only one species on that entire trip (this may be a mistake but it represents quite precisely my experience of it). There, hovering in numbers and clearly visible through the downpour of a chill late winter afternoon, with all their markings visible to the naked eye, were my life kittiwakes. They were peculiarly obliging, for kittiwakes are, after all, "only gulls," and after a while to the tired eye all gulls can seem to look alike, and rather commonplace at that. But unlike our all too common herring and black-backed gulls, which are both much larger and very happy to scavenge over the land, kittiwakes are "highly pelagic." They are slightly larger than the delicate Bonaparte's gull, but similarly marked in various of their phases. But these black-legged kittiwakes made it easy even for me, woozy with nausea and dulled with chill and dampness, to distinguish them. Many of them were first-year birds, boldly marked across the wings with a sharply contrasting "W" pattern easily visible even without binoculars. The lifebird dance would have to wait until we got to shore, where it was duly performed much later, but ironically, while the misery of that day is still vivid to my senses, my strongest memory is of those birds, seen with the wretchedness of chill and nausea, yet the best look I have had to this moment at kittiwakes.

So the question for me is whether it was worth it after all. Would I do it again? To my surprise, I feel myself saying, yes, it was worth it, yes, I might try it. The day was not entirely birdless, and that after all was the point. I never had illusions about nature or the sea. My relation to them both is love and fear. It's no surprise that one of the prices of loving is exposure to the fear. Darwin never hesitated to take risks and undergo discomfort in far more serious circumstances. I at least, some miles east of Cape May, on my way back to a motel, found my kittiwake.

ringed turtledove

RINGED TURTLE DOVE

I think it clever of the turtle
In such a fix to be so fertile.
—Ogden Nash

*T*HERE ARE MOMENTS in the field when the world seems
made of birds. A tree on a windless day suddenly seems
in motion as every leaf twists or sags to the movement of
small birds, some visible, some hidden, darting, hovering,
confusingly perceptible in their erratic motion in different degrees of focus. The problem then is not where the birds are, in
the upper branches, near the trunk, out on a limb—since they
are everywhere—but on which of the many figures in motion
the eye should concentrate, what losses might be incurred by
catching the warbler in the upper branches while several others are moving below, or by noting that flash of color rather
than this seductive movement, or by following a flight to an
adjoining tree. I have stood in a grove of trees in Central Park
on a Sunday morning in May embarrassed by avian plenty,

hearing Paul and other migrant birders calling the names of warblers, kinglets, gnatcatchers, vireos, birds I'm not seeing as I call "chestnut-sided," "red-start," "bay-breasted," or "black-poll."

Overwhelmed by riches, I feel on such occasions, although very briefly, that this is what birding is about, and it's entirely natural. Why should I have to struggle for the sight of a single bird, after long periods of slow stalking, when there are birds everywhere? There are spots, like that grove in Central Park, to which I routinely return, expecting to find abundance each time. In the woods near my home on another rich May morning, Michael guided me through muck I had always previously avoided to a grove alive with bird sound and movement, warblers and orioles and tanagers and kinglets and gnatcatchers, all, it seemed, actively waiting for me to identify them. I have been back to that spot dozens of times, on every visit to the woods, and it has never again, to my eyes, lived so intensely.

Wade, the true ornithologist among us, guaranteed me one May a cerulean warbler if we went with him to Bull's Island along the Delaware. It was not hard to persuade me since I had never seen a cerulean, and when we arrived the whole park had been transformed into an aviary. I have never seen so many scarlet tanagers—one a season will keep my need for bright colors satisfied; they were in virtually every tree. Wade led us to a spot near the canal where, he said, the cerulean would be waiting. It was. And it was visible enough and in enough company that I had time to check it against my field guide and note all the field marks. It was almost too easy. I asked myself whether I couldn't make every migration season a success just by coming to Bull's Island, where at the bridge all the local swallows were swerving and twisting, in the thick woods the flycatchers seemed all ready to announce themselves, in the groves the warblers, orioles, tanagers, kinglets, gnatcatchers were displaying as they fed. But after three or four years of seeking those birds in those places again, I no longer make Bull's Island an inevitable stop on my migration birding tours.

Abundant birding moments and places like that are rarities. There's a curious arbitrariness about where and when birds turn up, consistent with my general sense of the perversity of the natural world. Persistent birders and ornithologists can rely on certain patterns of movement, of feeding, of mating, of territoriality. But not even they can predict how any given place at any given moment will look. Wade wasn't exactly lucky when he predicted the cerulean, but the probability that it would be there because it had tended to be there in the past was only a probability. While there are reasons for the migrating birds to cluster so intensely in trees thick with blossoms and seeds as they fatten for the demanding flight north (they sometimes cluster even in a pin oak on my street, which by mid-May is rich with nourishment), there is no knowing when that will happen or if it will happen on your watch, or if they will always return to the same areas. Place is crucial, but like almost everything else in birding, it's not entirely predictable.

The natural moments of abundance imperceptibly devolve into natural moments of absence. Gazing excitedly at the abundant trees, I have found after five or ten minutes, without my being aware of it, the birds gradually get harder to locate, the movement diminishes, and suddenly I do become aware that I am looking only at trees and that it seems absurd to be standing there as though something were happening when all I am really trying to do is turn the leaves into the birds they were just minutes before.

In my experience, the emptiness is more characteristic than the abundance, but it is the abundance against which I tend to measure my birding trips. That is a mistake. After encounters with flocks of feeding migrants, it takes some time for me to come to terms with the fact that for long periods on most birding trips, I am lucky to find a new day's species or two in any given spot. I keep hoping that the next tree, the next pond, the next boggy grove will turn up the flycatchers I haven't seen today, and the warblers I have missed, and that elusive cuckoo. But if birding were that easy it couldn't be as pleasurable. When I express my disappointment about the absence of birds on one of our trips, Paul reminds me that we are having fun anyway. And of course he is right: the experience of bird austerity on field trips occurs in places I want to be, feel privileged to be, and under circumstances that are in themselves sufficient justification for the trip. And when, on those austere days, we find a single bird in some otherwise motionless tree, it is like a bonus.

Long stretches, even on our good birding days, are birdless, or, rather, without new birds for the day. These ostensible sterile patches are, however, fertile with the calming tensions of the quest, the intensification of the senses as ears tune for the faintest intimation of a song, for a twitter, for a warble, a squeak, or a chuck, and eyes strain at every movement that might not be caused by the wind or a falling seed or leaf. We learn, at Paul's injunction, not to point even when we want to communicate silently the presence of a bird, and I spend much time during our trips restraining my excitement so that I won't spook the very birds we are trying to see; we stealthily keep down the crackle of our steps through the underbrush; as we approach a pond through a thicket of phragmites, we need to make ourselves as invisible as possible, for the slightest sound and the slightest visual prominence will send the ducks, even already a hundred yards away, gliding quietly out of the range of binoculars. The difference between a leaf in thick foliage blown by the wind and a leaf shuddering abruptly from the motion of a hidden bird is often amazingly and decisively clear.

Birds transform places. Birding is a state of mind that makes where I am another kind of world. Driving through the quiet city at six in the morning on the way to some birding rendezvous, I have a sense both of all that mighty heart beating still and of its relation to that other heart, out in the wild, to which I am moving. On the way to the field and in it, even when the birds are not visible, I feel more completely alive than at any other time, less separate from the places I occupy, however anomalous my presence in a swamp or on a snowy and bitter cold beach may seem. Oddly, out in the places where I have no business—woods, marshes, sea shores, lakes, groves, fields, mountains—I find myself feeling much more integral with the world than when, in office, market, home, I am doing the work or taking the pleasures that have in effect defined me. With a pair of binoculars in my hands, just as there seem to be no ugly birds, so there seem to be no ugly places. I have birded places that most people would prefer not to visit, me too when I don't have my binoculars. Garbage dumps and landfills, for example, have their charms as long as the birds are abundant (and the hawks relish the rats that rummage in the waste) and the temperature is below freezing so that the stench is tolerable and the ground frozen. The visit to the local dump that inspired Michael's essay for the *Times* turned up not only several dozen red-tailed hawks, but a peregrine falcon sitting quietly near the entrance, a sharp-shinned hawk in the brush, a short-eared owl in an overgrown landfill, lots of horned larks, and several gorgeous red foxes, which can't be listed as birds but have their own mammalian attractions.

I have birded the streets of Palo Alto, where I have spotted great horned owls and my first red-naped woodpecker (thought at the time to be a mere variant of the yellow-bellied sapsucker). But I have gone downscale, too, along the grubby bay in Perth Amboy, where I saw my first Bonaparte's gull, and in the streets of Brooklyn, where I saw the spotted redshank, and along Route 1 south of New Brunswick, and at the high school in Highland Park, where I saw in the trees by the edge of the running track not one but two yellow-billed

cuckoos, a bird that I often spend whole seasons without seeing. Neighbors are not quite used to seeing me walk the streets
with binoculars, particularly in May, streets where I saw my
first rose-breasted grosbeak, with its startlingly beautiful scarlet V-neck, and where I get a sense each May morning of
whether there has been a new wave of migrants through during the previous night, and where an Eastern wood peewee
settles in, hidden in trees in my neighbor's much larger yard. I
have learned the call of the titmouse by chasing down a "peter,
peter, peter" across about a half mile of roads behind the college and finally spotting the bird in the act of singing. I have
seen a red-tailed hawk circling with majestic confidence in the
rightness of his place over downtown Toronto.

One does not need the wilderness for birds. Birding turns
cities into wilderness, a place that its citizens barely know.
One does not need groves bursting with birdlife. The world's
metamorphosis when I'm out birding makes any place magical. I always have the sense of carrying an open secret, one
available to everyone who chooses to look, but in fact known
only to me and my birding colleagues. It gives me a purchase
on city streets and city parks that people who live there and
know them far better than I do not have. Sometimes, the
more unlikely the spot, the more richly the significance of
birds comes home to me, the more clearly I understand that
the cities were once places where non-human life felt at home
and even now remain places where that life will reassert itself
wherever the slightest niche or crevice or crack allows it. My
brother claims that when he was a boy, peregrine falcons were
frequently visible on city rooftops. The recent project to re-
store peregrines has brought some of those birds back to the
city, although I still haven't seen them there.

The world seen through bird binoculars is like those vast
parking lots, smooth and suburban, filling daily with cars,
which slowly, inevitably break out in burst veins of cracks,
through which grass and weeds keep pushing as though they

have been waiting, half smothered, for the opportunity, while no blacktopping, no traffic, no Christmas shopping days can really kill them. So Central Park becomes birdland for anyone willing to look. The birds make places new and are for me constant reminders of some alternative life that most people don't have to know but that sustains itself even where humans have taken over completely and that is secretly driving their green age as well. It puts me in on a secret, makes the city a giant tree alive with wild movement that those in the midst of its wildness cannot know. It's ironic that an area of just a few square blocks in Central Park is probably the best place in a hundred-mile radius to observe migrant birds during the spring. In the boathouse by the lake, just on the edge of the Ramble, birders used to hang a birding notebook that only other birders and, I suppose, the restaurant owner, knew existed. I used to check it with delight each visit to the park, in on another secret, learning about some of the birding wonders of the Ramble and the comic self-consciousness of others in on the cabal. So I take my birding pleasures where I can and I don't need those abundant trees and those stunning moments in which more birds than I can count are swarming, hovering, diving, fluttering, sitting, singing on picturesque branches in remote and romantically beautiful places.

One of my most remarkable and yet banal sightings came when I set out to find the ringed turtle dove, a bird I had always thought of as belonging to the Song of Solomon, madrigals, and renaissance love poetry. It was on a business visit to Los Angeles, and I had happened to read that the ringed turtle dove, a very difficult bird to find outside of cages, had established itself in a tiny park in downtown L.A. I had no time for serious birding and was forced to spend almost all of my time inside a terrifying modern luxury hotel from which I could never find a street exit.

I was skeptical about the turtle dove but determined to look. All of the books noted that it was a bird that had not established itself in America (that still belonged in English renaissance poetry, I thought), but that was occasionally to be found in city parks. It was definitely not in Central Park, where lots of other genuinely wild birds regularly turned up. I decided to take seriously the literature that pointed to the small urban park adjoining the library in downtown L.A. where the doves had established themselves and could be counted on, and broke free of the hotel.

I went with some friends who helped me find an exit but who were not very interested in birds, only bemused by my claim that I was seeking a birding rarity in downtown L.A. I went without binoculars, which seemed in that context inappropriate, and as it turned out I didn't need them. The "park" might have been more accurately described as an urban dump. Virtually no grass was left, only litter, old paper, shards of decaying food, broken bottles, derelicts' bedding, a few skimpy looking trees. I got anxious in my middle-class way as we approached the place, which was only a few blocks from the hotel, but it was so small, less than a square block, and there were so few people around, that it seemed silly to worry. There certainly were no other birders out for the rarity.

My skepticism intensified. Why would any bird that couldn't establish itself in more congenial places want to live here? Where were the inevitable birders such a rarity should have attracted? And how could a rarity be so permanently in an easily accessible spot? It was the kind of place in which I expected to find pigeons or maybe even mourning doves, but that bird of love and romance, the turtle dove? Yet there it was. Or rather, there they were, seeming as predictable as pigeons. Utterly at home sitting on branches of the few trees or grazing, as doves are wont, on the spare vegetation and the debris, they hardly seemed "rare." But there could be no mistake. Though in most respects shaped like mourning doves, they were lighter, silvery-gray, and they had that distinctive black collar on the backs of their necks, and they were a lot prettier than urban habitués of derelict parks ought to be.

I wasn't going to check for any other unusual birds. Nothing else would hang out here. Madrigals and the Song of Solomon would never be the same for me. But I showed this lifebird to my friends, who were distinctly unimpressed (I was too embarrassed to do my lifebird dance). They conceded without enthusiasm that those birds probably didn't look exactly like other doves in other parks they had known, but I knew they did look like urban birds and did not call attention to themselves. I would have guessed that the urban passersby simply took them for granted as part of the place and didn't know they weren't pigeons or any of the common American doves.

Later, still fascinated by my secret, I did a little research only to find out to my disappointment that there really are lots of different species of turtle doves and that this was pretty certainly not the turtle dove of poetic fame. That dove, the *streptopelia turtur*, is common in central Europe. The ringed turtle dove, *streptopelia risoria*, is probably originally an African bird. No matter: "turtle dove" carries with it the weight of Biblical romance and my non-birding friends weren't terribly interested anyway.

There was nothing in the scene for them that could explain my excitement and exuberance. Those "exotic" birds didn't feel exotic. This was not a place to hang out. It was hardly a site of scenic wonder. Certainly, it was difficult to imagine our quest from the hotel through the city streets as a journey equivalent to those characteristic of TV nature shows telling the story of ecologically impelled hunts for rare species, and in which so much depends on the glamour of place and the strangeness of the animals. Yet these were, indeed, descendants of Old World birds that were at least closely related to birds that had captured the imagination of poets for millennia. Their ancestors had probably escaped from cages and managed to survive in the urban wild and create enough generations of descendants to satisfy the listing criteria of the

ABA. That the doves found downtown L.A. compatible was hardly a mark against them. For me, they in their urban casualness made the unattractive urban conglomeration something new and wild. Sitting unselfconsciously on scraggly branches above refuse and grassless turf, they were as much a reason to marvel at the variations and aberrations and diversity of bird life as those trees teeming with birds in woods and wilderness and, yes, Central Park. As *The Audubon Society Encyclopedia of North American Birds* tersely but wonderfully puts it, the ringed turtle dove "has established itself as a free-living bird in downtown Los Angeles." And if we are thinking about rarity, "free-living" turtle doves in downtown L.A. are probably more impressively significant of the vitality of the earth than those abundant trees in migration season, and like good urban dwellers who punch the clock and work through their daily routines, much more predictable.

lapwing

LAPWING

*I*T TURNED OUT TO BE, as we might have expected, the coldest weekend of the winter thus far. But this was a weekend planned months ahead, and so late on Friday evening I prepared the gorp that would provide the calories to heat us through long stretches in the car and out on remote beaches and backwaters of Long Island (if any part of Long Island might be considered remote). The bagels sliced, the Sorels brought up from the basement, the REI underwear prepared to seal the heat in and let moisture out, the telescope checked, binoculars, National Geographic guide, croaker to keep my glasses from falling off, several layers of clothing, cap and, of course, coffee (decaf) prepared for the thermos: everything seemed to be ready. The rituals were familiar, and I sank to sleep with visions of scoters sweeping the point at Montauk, and grebes and loons and eider ducks bobbing miraculously on the rough surf, disappearing behind, reemerging on top of wildly disorganized rollings of the sea.

Perhaps because I knew pretty well what we would be seeing, the anticipation had less of the excitement of exploration,
more of the satisfaction of ritual and austerely comfortable
fulfillment. I realized that much of what I was anticipating
was reentrance into a community that, put simply, made me
feel good and that, for two days, had nothing to do with the
responsibilities, the people, the places that mark my everyday
life. Paul would be quiet, gentle, warm, full of interesting facts
about birds and his latest reading in natural history, and so
certain of taking pleasure in the deep frost and the sightings,
abundant or scarce, that I felt assured of shared pleasure even
if those expected sea ducks didn't turn up and the frozen lakes
gleamed birdless in the chill, and the wind tore through my
protection out there at Montauk Point.

Michael had decided to come along after all, and while for
him this had become something of a sacrifice, his being there
would be an important part of the pleasure for Paul and me. I
could only assume that he ventured into inevitable discomfort
because there was warmth in the relationships if not in the air;
and perhaps it all would be worth it to him because of the familiar comforts of nature talk and friendly concern and ritual
dinner at the Shagamut Restaurant (the only one open this
time of year out at Montauk). I took a probably silly pleasure
in knowing that everyone was expecting my unusual gorp
spiced with exotic Indian hot snacks and my bagels with lox
and cream cheese, which somehow tasted spectacularly good
after a particularly bitter encounter with winter on some exposed spot way east on Long Island.

I realized, in the midst of my normal enthusiasm for the
winter birds (an enthusiasm cynical friends might have
thought merely rehearsed) that almost everything difficult
about this trip provided part of the pleasure. I remembered,
not with unqualified nostalgia, what it felt like to stand out
there at the Point before dawn with the temperature well below 20 degrees and with the wind finding whatever mistakes I

had made in preparing for the cold, and with the well pro-
tected toes first growing painful and then starting to numb,
and with the almost intolerable sharpness of cold in the fin-
gers as they gradually lose control over the focus knob on the
binoculars. And yet, of course, reporting that painful pleasure
to incredulous friends was often worth the pain. The discomforts of Montauk are part of my imagination of myself. I
bought my Sorels because of those annual two hours. And my
trips to the Salt Lake City REI, where otherwise I would have
felt myself a fraud among young backpackers and awesomely
skilled climbers, were largely inspired by my anticipation of
annual mornings at Montauk.

And then, there was the memory of sharing pain with
friends and not flinching or moaning or complaining but
finding some kind of warmth in managing to pick out the
Bonaparte gulls, graceful, pointy winged, bold, triangular
white showing in the primaries, sleek and rapid, from among
the larger gulls—herring and black-backed—who seemed
relatively unperturbed as they held slow and steady and graceful, too, against the wind in the diminishing darkness. There
was warmth of a kind, too, in beginning to tell the difference
among white-winged scoters and black scoters and surf scoters, all black and barely recognizable in the pre-dawn light as
they flew with duck-rapid wings low over the water at least a
hundred yards away. It's a very odd pleasure, as I anticipate
and remember it, and yet it's undeniably a pleasure. It probably wouldn't be if I were to do it alone.

The Point is, of course, the climax of this annual winter
trip, annually conducted somehow on the coldest days of the
year. But, because we are pretty sure what we will see out
there on the Point, our pilgrimage to it becomes an excuse for
other things, as well. Some of the most interesting birding experiences of the trip and often of the year come, unexpectedly,
at stops along the way through eastern Long Island. Traveling
out that far so long after the "season" puts us in an exclusive if

rather shaggy society. The whole of the island, from Riverhead to Montauk, can become a large birding club, a community of people who don't know each other and are otherwise indistinguishable from the general island population, and who yet recognize each other immediately, feel free to start conversations, give advice, ask questions. It was at the Point, several years before, that we met "Andy," whom we had come to expect on each of our annual trips out there ever since and who not only possessed a superb Kowa scope, much better than any of our optics, but who had much better eyes and could pick alcids out from the scoter runs, find the gannets glittering and diving in the early morning sun far out on the ocean, and could tell a king from a common eider without hesitation. He was pleased to know and see more than we did, but he was more pleased to help us see, and he was fun to talk to. It was Andy who pointed out to me my "life" snowy owl, at which I had been looking puzzled, intent, unsure, for quite a while before he arrived. Paul and I talked about Andy and were looking forward to finding him again, learning from him again, somewhere on our way east to Montauk. In fact, Andy didn't turn up this time, and we ended by needing other scope-bearing friends.

With my gorp and bagels in hand, and without for this once forgetting anything, and with my new gloves guaranteed to keep off the pain of the Montauk dawn, we had made our first stop at Jones Beach, where Paul and I had often found surprises, like a catbird, shivering in the bare parking lot bushes, or like the long-eared owl that awaited us as we descended from the lookout tower. This time, to our astonishment, a tree swallow, summery and flittering, white belly contrasting distinctively with its dark back, took off from a frozen pond in search of what possible insects. There weren't many birds around, but Paul and I were already delighted with this first winter aberration, and feeling very good despite an early failure (a distant white blob picked out from the ob-

servation tower remained inaccessible and unidentified, however hard we worked to maneuver the marshes and turn it
into another snowy owl). And as we moved off farther east
with only a few winter species and that one remarkable summer swallow behind, we all chewed contentedly on bagels with
lox and cheese. It was, I confess, a relief to be back in the car,
out of the wind and the deep frost, eating the bagels, sipping
the coffee, talking birds and family and Michael's new romance and a new book about sexual selection, and then, giving the wheel to Michael, allowing myself to drowse to the
familiar voices saying probably interesting things about a
book I hadn't yet read.

We pushed on toward Bridgehampton, twenty miles short
of Montauk, where a sandhill crane had been spotted out at
Sag Pond. We consulted the instructions Paul had copied off
the rare bird alert, which now was accessible not only by
phone but through an e-mail list to which a vast and quiet
community of birders attends religiously. Somehow I found
myself excited at the idea of locating a single sandhill here on
Long Island although I had seen probably half a million
sandhills near Grand Island, Nebraska the preceding March.
Alerts of this kind, announcing the presence of a bird that
shouldn't be where you are, inevitably produce a large birding
society and force the recognition that this eccentric's activity
that ostensibly puts birders in touch not with society but with
the non-human, natural world is deeply social. Someone spots
an unusual bird and within hours thousands of people know
about it, know exactly where it is, travel miles to find it, do
find it. There's a society behind every rare bird.

Paul, Michael, and I are not likely to change our daily routines to chase down such aberrant birds and join the birding
community that forms itself around it, but when we are in
our birding mode (if the birds are anywhere near our routes)
we find such alerts irresistible. So we had planned the day's
trip in such a way that we would get to Sag Pond with plenty

of afternoon light left and seek out the sandhill, number 500,001 for me.

For a short, delusive time, I felt like an expert, was ready to point out likely habitats for sandhills, to talk about sandhill behavior, to recall my recent intensive engagement with this bird's extended family. But as we were driving down a back lane, no cars visible, quiet, exurban, chilly and bright and prosperous looking, a van came up the road we were looking for. The driver of the van slowed at the turn and peered into our car where we three sat, already looking grubby and un-kempt, with bearded and grubby Paul distinctly visible in the front seat: we watched as he rolled down the van window, clearly wanting to say something to us. As we slowed in re-sponse, Michael punching the button to open his window, the driver called to us: "Looking for the sandhill?"

Even as he said it, we were all thinking how absurd and wonderful the moment was. Why, on this obscure back road, was there nothing menacing in his strange behavior? What could that question have meant to anyone not there for the birds? How did he know—was it Paul's obvious birdy grubbi-ness?—that we would know what he was asking? Why was he so sure that he didn't have to add the "crane"? And how could he so confidently use "the," as though this one particular bird was on everyone's mind. Obviously, by equipment, clothing, generally grubby appearance, we belonged to the community that knew the language.

"Yeah," we all shouted. "Follow me," he called back. He slid the window up and drove down that narrow exurban lane so fast that in turning to follow him we almost lost him. There was a car behind him, another birder, clearly, who had re-ceived a similar invitation, and off we went, a caravan of three, too fast down the narrow road. We were laughing to and at ourselves as we followed, and I, at least, was deeply skeptical about actually seeing the sandhill where we were go-ing because if it had flown across Sag Pond some time before, it wasn't likely to be standing exposed and visible in that same place by the time we arrived. But it didn't matter: here we were not invisible but self-evidently "birders," part of a small mob of sandhill pursuers, joining in a birding chase that would be pretty hard not to notice. It was silly, funny, pleasurable. And, of course, it would have been nice if the bird were to be there.

It wasn't. The driver of the van said he had seen it under that tree from the other side of the pond just fifteen minutes before. But there was nothing under the tree and it was clearly private property, so we weren't going to march across it to see if the bird had moved behind the house or if it were visible from there at some other spot on the pond. The rare bird alert had said the crane was staying around the pond and the van driver seemed to confirm it. The alert also said to be aware that this part of the pond was private property. And of course, birders who care about the activity more than they care about their lists are extremely careful about private property, and about not annoying people by violating their privacy, thus bringing wealthy wrath down on the community of birding enthusiasts. We were in fact lucky because later we learned that at the same spot, an irate property owner had attacked— like Betsey Trotwood after the donkeys in *David Copperfield*— another gathering of cars and people who, perhaps, had been a little less considerate of privacy. I thought we were being egregious enough, and so with no crane visible nor likely to appear, we abandoned the little society of people swapping information about sandhill cranes and this elusive one in particular, and drove back toward where we had been diverted by the driver of the van.

We checked out the mudflats on the pond, the sorts of places where sandhills like to rest during the night. With less than an hour to sunset, we expected the crane would likely arrive shortly, but waiting was chancy and very chilly. The Long Island rarity was perhaps not, after all, worth the wait in the cold where no other birds were visible, and there was just time to squeeze in a little more birding before dark and before we got to Montauk and dinner at the Shagamut, which the sustained chill in our bones was making increasingly attractive. So after a little consultation with yet another group of birders who had come for the sandhill and not found it, we went off craneless but at least amused.

The Shagamut Restaurant, which always figured importantly in our imaginations of this trip, seemed to have undergone a transformation, for while we were first struck by the much higher food prices on the new menu, we were then struck by the high quality of the food. The new prices were really legitimate then, and to our surprise, dinner was not the austere pleasure we normally associate with birding restaurants, but almost luxuriant. Montauk outings had no right to be luxuriant, but everyone was happy, particularly Michael, for whom the fish on the dish was considerably more important than the birds he knew we would be likely to see during the trial at the Point the next morning. So we relished the Shagamut as long as we could and then headed back to our rather austere but not uncomfortable motel, whose gas heating flamed visibly under a red hot grate just outside one of the bedrooms.

Birds had, in a way, been the smallest part of a day that had offered alternative pleasures. Sitting around in long johns and disrepair, we might have been let down when we discovered that our first day bird tally was an alarmingly small twenty-eight species. I really didn't mind and didn't need to whip myself to enthusiasm about the one undoubted birding success of the day: the tree swallow. It was good being there in this shabby room with the gas fire audible and virtually all the faucets and switches on the verge of disfunction. It was a long winter night and we sat around cozily talking about the likely trials of the morning. No pre-dawn breakfast spot would be open, but there were still some bagels left. Paul had some pastries. We got some coffee for morning warming. We would survive. The birds subsided from the center of our attention as we talked, as a group, of ways to make do.

So we did. The Point was even colder than we had anticipated because the wind was even stronger (but my Sorels actually kept my feet painless); the gloves did no better than any other gloves I had worn out there. Worst, however, we watched the smallest flight of scoters we had ever seen on clear Montauk mornings. And we stood precariously on the hill overlooking the ocean, a hill that had eroded so much during the past year that the path we used to stand on barely existed anymore. The scope wouldn't stand against the wind, and so we were left to use only our binoculars on birds far too distant, until we realized we would be better off below on the beach proper.

Those are moments for which one pays a price, this time in chill and relative birdlessness, but the dawn, in the deep of winter, rising warmly out of a bank of purple clouds flat against the horizon, and gradually making the few scoters rustily visible, mixing those Turneresque colors and seeming to grow with a quiet indifference and authority vastly over the waters, was worth the price. Why that inhuman silence and show of color should make me feel good when it does nothing to warm the air and I'm doing all I can to keep from admitting I'm miserable and my nose is leaking uncontrollably, I don't know. It did. Part of it had to do with the realization that this wasn't happening to me alone. It was having the same effect on Paul. Michael, who was too smart to stand still up there looking out on the ocean, was moving rapidly down the beach, resisting the discomfort but surely feeling the overwhelming presence of the sun. There were seals playing where the birds might have been. It was hard for any of us not to be looking at them when we should have been looking for the birds. This was, in all its austerity, our place: nobody else was around. Something quite wonderful was happening, even without the birds, but not without friends.

We finally gave up on the birds, for although they did come in the hundreds—scattered groups of ten and fifteen at a time—they were already thinning out, as they do even on the best of birding days after an hour or two of sunlight. We headed back to Montauk where, at last, a breakfast place was open. Grubby and chilled through, we rushed in, settled down, worked our way through waffles and coffee and warmth and the waking of a community, with noisy children and local gossip, that didn't seem much concerned with birds. That's always an odd feeling: to have focussed intensely on a world immediately impinging on the local community but not at all in that community's consciousness. It's disorienting, and yet within our little community, a source of unspoken pride.

But as we were sipping our last cups of coffee, a young man called from our world and another table: "Did you see anything interesting?" Identified again. Back in the larger community again. No, we hadn't seen anything interesting this morning, but we did see a tree swallow yesterday at Jones Beach. Interesting enough, but, having identified us as birders, the stranger had something important he wanted to tell us, and he walked over to the table.

"I saw a northern lapwing." "Wow," I said. Really? A lapwing? Where? That's the response he wanted—and deserved. He was a birder we instinctively knew we could trust. This was no fantasy or macho affirmation of birding powers. He wanted us to see the bird. And, very carefully, he described where he had seen it and how to get there. We took the instructions down on a napkin and changed our itinerary for the return trip west in an instant. We were pleased to have been spotted once again as part of that floating birding community that makes for connection and trust wherever one goes with binoculars.

It was at the intersection of Halsey and Mecox road, in Bridgehampton, in fact not terribly far from where we failed to see the sandhill the day before. We knew that the lapwing was yet more rare than the sandhill, but my instinctive pessimism informed me that we would miss this bird too. Pessimism is, of course, a protection from the pain of not getting what I want, and I was still more than secretly thrilled at the very possibility of seeing the lapwing. The only place I had ever seen lapwings was in England, where they are pretty common.

They are strange, beautiful European birds, actually shore birds, part of the plover family, but as likely as our killdeer to be seen quite some distance away from the water, in flat fields grazing. They are pretty large, a couple of inches bigger than killdeer, more striking although not, strictly, colorful. When you see them well they have crazy crests sticking up like loose hairs, but firmly. They are boldly marked, with a clear black breast under white neck and above white belly. Wings are dark and seem almost black although, apparently (and I have never seen them in such a light) they can be a glossy green. In flight, the wings are pretty broad for a shore bird, and from beneath they show sharply defined white linings behind the black. So if you see them, you know you have seen them.

We were hoping for the sighting as we drove again onto the back roads off the southern shore of eastern Long Island. Again, the roads were empty, the houses expensive and trim, the sun bright, the air very cold, and the lawns well groomed. The instructions were careful, and we zigged and zagged where we were supposed to, hoping that we would find the field and the white picket fence that marked the place where our Montauk acquaintance claimed to have seen the bird. No problem: the word was out: there, indeed, was the birding community once more. A dozen cars were parked erratically just off the narrow roads and a congregation of birdy folk was standing around telescopes and talking—but, alas, clearly not looking at anything in particular. This was—or had been—the spot.

Everyone was eager to talk about it. Yes, it was just there. It had flown off to the right to a spot, they expected, to which it had been moving consistently since the time it had first been identified where we were standing. Some people, who were satisfied that they had seen it, were packing up, cramming scopes into vans. An elderly gentleman came over to give us precise instructions about how to look for it, where to find it. He was almost too helpful, because Paul, Michael and I were eager to get over to the other field, about a half mile down the road, to which, we were being informed, the lapwing regularly flew. At last, tired of being helpful, the gentleman shambled over to his waiting wife, scope over his shoulder, pleased with having seen the bird and pleased with having established himself as an authority on it. We were not ungrateful.

But we rushed to the car and followed several people to the alternative spot, another field, more broadly accessible and not fenced in. There were yet more of the astonishing large community that had managed to gather for the lapwing within hours of its first identification by the man we met in the restaurant. Another dozen or so cars were parked in a long line at the edge of a cornfield, and there was another crowd of birders, some of whom had just seen it, some of whom were being told where it had landed, in the old cornfield.

Desire began to win out over protective pessimism. We were so close, so hot in pursuit, I began to think we really had a chance to see it. And so Michael moved off in one direction, still at the wheel of the car, Paul and I walked forward, behind three or four other people, into the field. Paul's sense of birding propriety made it difficult even to step onto the field, but behind other trespassers, he compromised. How, I wondered—my mind on the bird and not, I fear, on civility—could we possibly see the bird if it were hunkered down among the old yellowed husks. But we were too close not to try, and we moved slowly, as quietly as we could, about ten paces toward the field when suddenly, "There it is," someone called. And there it was.

Several thousand miles from where it should be, the north-ern lapwing seemed to leap from the field, displaying the boldness of its marking, the sharp white wing linings against the dark distinctively broad wings, the almost wiggling, erratic flight—clean across the line of our vision, slowly up higher, twisting off to the right toward the field from which we had just come, where the rest of the community of birders that day was waiting for its return. It displayed itself unmistakably, boldly, twisting, being a northern lapwing, and thrilling this large heterogeneous community of birders, standing half a mile apart, making our Montauk day better than we could have imagined if all the scoters had been out there where we thought they would be at dawn. In the sky above us all, but not too high, twisting our separate sightings into one, the northern lapwing gave us reason for sticking together.

The following day, in an e-mail message, subject: "Wow," Paul informed me that his reference book showed that the northern lapwing had been spotted in this part of the world only three times in this century. A week later, Michael, who had suffered the winter discomforts of eastern Long Island with unspoken misery for two days, cramped in a car much of that time, chilled and birdless when he got out, confessed that he too had been thrilled by the sight of that wonderfully obliging and boldly beautiful bird so terribly off course and so deeply the source of a communal and yet entirely private hap-piness that bitter Sunday morning.

common yellowthroat

YELLOWTHROAT

*T*HE *YELLOWTHROAT* is a little warbler that stays low in the bushes and sings loudly, "tawitchity, witchity, witchity witch." That at least is what I hear. Peterson's version, which must certainly be the ultimate origin of mine, is very close: "witchity-witchity-witchity-witch; sometimes witchy-witchy-witchy-witch." Other representations of that voice, which on a bright spring morning enlivens the fields around, play minor variations on the "witchity" theme. In a world of subtle differences and endless divergences, the yellowthroat produces a clear consensus on what, to the human ear, it sounds like. Michael, who has a knack for encapsulating a bird's identity in a word or a phrase and who wonderfully called the hooded warbler "the Lone Ranger," calls the yellowthroat simply and reasonably, the "witchity bird."

For other reasons, Paul calls it "el bandito." If the voice is striking, the face of the mature male is yet more so. The bird's dark eyes peer out from a sharply defined black mask, outlined above in white, which marks it off from the uniform olive back. Beneath the mask, the throat and part of the belly run to a brilliant yellow (in the East, the lower belly tends to fade into white). There is something comic and cheering in finding that masked face staring out at you from behind the branches of low brush, making sure that you are not threatening its territory. El bandito is not quiet about his space and will "chuck" and chip at you until you leave. The pleasure in such a bird has a lot to do with the way it confirms its identity unambiguously in every respect: both voice and mask testify without question to that identity. You could hang a poster in the post office and you would have to pay the reward many times over. No ambiguities, no subtleties of distinction. The disguise of the mask is the mark of identity.

In my part of the world at least the yellowthroat is one of the most common of the warblers, and since it stays around after migration to nest, I hear its voice right through the summer. It's a steady companion and one of those birds that makes introducing friends to the world of birding an immediate pleasure. When they catch sight of that mask they are likely to fall in love immediately (unless, of course, they are incorrigibly cynical about birdwatching). And the voice makes it easy to convince people that one can discriminate birdsong: "tawitchity, wichity, wichity, witch" distinguishes it from all other birds.

But birding is rarely less complicated than life. There are a couple of problems with the common yellowthroat. One is relatively simple and is the result of nomenclature rather than of difficulties of visual or aural discrimination. While the yellowthroat is very much a warbler and while it does indeed have a yellow throat, it is not the "yellow-throated warbler." The arbitrariness of bird naming in this case is pretty clear since there are quite a few warblers with yellow throats—the Kentucky, the Canada, the magnolia, the prairie (sort of, since it also has some striping on the sides of the throat), just to name a few. Then there is the "yellow-throated warbler," which, of course, has a yellow throat too. Language needs to make distinctions and rich as it is, it isn't equal to the sorts of distinctions it would have to make if it were to keep up with the relentless indifference of nature to "natural" categories.

I take the arbitrariness of naming as part of the pleasure of birding, a continuing revelation of the ways in which "nature" and human conventions and consciousness are always inter-mingled and never in entirely satisfactory relation. The plea-sure of the mature male yellowthroat, in its striking distinctiveness, is an aberration in the scheme of things, if scheme is what it should be called. One of the reasons birding is so endlessly fascinating for me is that it constantly tempts me with the possibility of naming, classification, order, and constantly resists my impulses to make things make sense. It fills my mind with details that are shamefully inadequate not only to the details of the world I am trying to encounter but to what it is that serious birders know already. Yet I am always surprised to know how much I know—that I can speak with-out reference books or even birding tapes of the way yel-lowthroats look and sound, for example. Part of my problem in writing about birds is that I have to resist the temptation, which I deliberately choose not to do in this discussion of the yellowthroat, to load the page with miscellaneous facts that have somehow through the years, through field guides and field trips and discussions in Central Park and newspaper clippings and nature shows and bird books come to fill certain corners of my loosely organized mind. I often wonder how it is that when I go on field trips, even for several days, my friends and I can talk virtually nonstop about birds, unself-consciously, pleasurably, and always with a sense that we don't know enough. It's easy.

So take, for example, the connection, or non-connection, between the yellowthroat and the yellow-throated warbler. The latter is an entirely different bird in every way: appearance, habits, voice. What it shares with the yellowthroat is a yellow throat. But the yellow-throated warbler is not olive but gray black. It has white wing bars where the yellowthroat has none at all. Belly and underparts are white. It has a white eyeline on its black face. It hangs out not low in bushes and shrubs but usually high in tall trees, particularly pine. I get to see yellow-throated warblers only when I make a point of finding their appropriate habitat, and then only sometimes. They don't nest in my immediate area. Of course they are very pretty, but then I find it difficult not to think of almost every bird as very pretty in its own peculiar way. Its voice is not as distinctive as the yellowthroat's and I have trouble remembering it. I can't now, for example, produce a mnemonic version of it without checking the bird guides, although I think I would recognize it if I heard it. Only the yellow throat connects these two distinctive birds. I have never met anyone who confused them in the field.

Another way in which yellowthroats manage to complicate the visual world instead of—like the mature masked male—simplifying it is that the female and immature yellowthroats are not at all easy to identify. If you look at that wonderful and despair-inducing page in Peterson—"Confusing Fall Warblers"—you will get some sense of the problem. In the fall the marvelous colors of so many of the American warblers seem to fall away. The stunningly contrasted black-throated blue warbler, for example, fades to a dark olive wash and Peterson has to point some pretty significant diagnostic arrows at tiny marks—a usually visible white wing patch, a "dark-cheeked" look—in order to distinguish it from a half dozen other washed-out warblers who would have been immediately recognizable in the spring. The female yellowthroat turns up on that page of "CFWs," as we call them, looking just like the prothonotary and mistakable for several others if you're not very careful. I have frequently in the field called yellowthroats "Nashville" until—if the bird is good enough to hang around—some expert shows me that there's a touch of white on the yellowthroat's underbelly that wouldn't be on the Nashville, or that the eye ring on the yellowthroat isn't complete and isn't really white, the way it would be on the Nashville. CFWs absorb the once distinctive yellowthroat and tell me what the birding world is really like.

And how about that unmistakable voice? It is easy to sustain the illusion that every bird has its distinctive song and that once you have that you "have" the bird. This is partially true, but of course it doesn't take much reflection to realize that birds must have distinctive *individual* voices. As they mark their spring nesting territories, they claim their spaces by sounding different to each other. Occasionally, they sound different to me, but it is true that birds tend to have relatively limited repertoires, usually much larger than I am aware of, but limited enough to be generally identifiable. There was, as counter example, a famous prairie warbler in an area in Cape May that sang in the same spot for several years. When Paul, Michael and I first heard it, we were pretty sure that there was a Kentucky warbler in the area, a bird whose voice is far closer to that of the Carolina wren than of the prairie warbler. Kentuckys are skulkers in the low dense brush of difficult damp places, and since we don't get to see them very often, we worked very hard to find this one. It might have been a half hour of hunting, following the elusive voice that emerged from the edge of a woods, before we finally saw the bird making the sound—and it was a prairie warbler, unmistakably. The prairie, which has a beautiful ascending, high voice that never stops rising, is another of my favorite birds, but it was shocking to see it singing in tones so different from its own.

I've never caught so aberrant a yellowthroat. It does "witchity" on and on and provides reassuring solace when I am struggling with other more difficult sounds. But it doesn't always sing the full witchity, and on many occasions I have found myself identifying a yellowthroat as a yellow warbler, a yellow warbler as a yellowthroat. Now the yellow warbler, an-other very common nesting warbler in my area, has its own "distinctive" voice. It is usually sharp and assertive and bright in a very different way from that of the yellowthroat. Once in Central Park, when I was chasing down such a bright sound, an experienced New York birder told me to listen for "kiss, kiss, kiss, gimme a kiss." I hear it now all the time and it has made the yellow warbler available to me in a peculiarly happy way. Sometimes it's only a fragment of the song, just, for ex-ample, "gimme a kiss." Sometimes there are a lot more kisses in it. But my mind is full of the rhythms of that command and I am pretty good at disentangling yellow warbler sound from other birds. Peterson is, for once, somewhat disappoint-ing on the yellow warbler's call: "tsee-tsee-tsee-tsee-titi-wee." The *National Geographic* guide renders it, "sweet, sweet, sweet, I'm so sweet." Not bad, but not as good as a kiss.

But these mnemonics disguise similarities in semantic dif-ferences. Although there is a rolling quality to a "wichity" that there isn't in a "kiss, kiss, kiss," the two sounds are a lot closer together than they seem on the printed page. And with atten-tion relaxed or the song fragmentary or varied with the aber-ration of sheer avian individuality, those songs can be mistaken for each other sometimes too. I'm not sure I know the whole repertoire of either of these birds. But right now, right outside my window, as I type and struggle to transfer the birding experience to the page, there's a bird begging for a kiss. "Gimme a kiss," he is insisting. And I'm pretty sure I know what he looks like. Pretty sure.

So maybe half the fun of birding is the sheer complication of birding life and the hopeless efforts of representation with which every birder, not only Peterson, bird guide writers, and ornithologists, must struggle. The other half remains the bird and the experience of it, the source I hope of the passion that drives my excursions into radical discomfort, and drives these efforts now, exercised in part against my better judgment of what the birding experience has meant to me all these years, to represent the birds and my life with them.

I can never repay the yellowthroat. It is one of the first warbler voices I hear every spring; until I hear it, I don't feel that the spring has legitimately begun. As the season progresses I encounter yellowthroats with greater frequency and their voices fill the wood margins with cheery tawichitys. I know that they are not really "cheery." It's all part of yellowthroat business, but why should I deny the sensation of cheer that it produces, willy nilly. Knowing and experiencing do not always coincide. I know for instance that the catbird, another ubiquitous spring visitor and summer nester, is not trying to be amusing. But standing in the early spring near a bush in which a catbird is sitting, for once not visible, and hearing its crazy and irregular repertoire of squeaks, whistles, peeps, and squawks interrupted by a distinctive call of a cat, I often find it impossible not to laugh. And there I am in a field alone giggling sometimes uncontrollably at the incongruous sounds of a bird that is only doing its mating job. It's a rite of spring, like the witchitying of the yellowthroat, which isn't quite so funny but is much more beautiful.

Although the yellowthroat doesn't know it, we have a fairly familiar and fond relationship. I have talked to it. It has chucked at me and followed me noisily along paths through the brush, making sure I am not going to intrude too far on its nesting privacies. It stares at me curiously from behind its disguise. It greets me each visit at the margin of the woods, and when it doesn't I know that the season hasn't begun or that it's ending.

And one day in mid-April a few years ago, when the winter was still doing its work on my mind and all the business it had left behind was occupying me anxiously, I went out for a Sunday jog in the park. It was my longest run—always reserved for Sundays—three miles out, three miles back to Tabatchnik's and bagels. As I ran I felt something of the release that comes from physical exertion, but my mind remained full of deadlines, papers to read and write, exams to give, reports to submit. It was chilly but bright. At the turnaround point in my run, a spot where the path dead-ends at the edge of a scrubby and wooded patch, I heard a sound unheard for more than six months, which didn't quite work its way into my consciousness, preoccupied as it was with responsibilities and winter. But the sound came again, unexpectedly, unmistakably. It was notice that the world was proceeding without my attention, almost behind my back, as I kept to the front the anxieties of work and family that had seemed so overwhelmingly large during the winter. It had nothing and everything to do with me: "tawitchity, witchity, witchity witch; tawitchity, witchity, witchity, witch." No confusions with other birdsong, of which there had been very little through the cold months. Without warning the bird had returned. Without warning, absurd as it was, I felt tears. I stopped, peered into the brush at the margin of the woods. Nothing to be seen. "Tawitchity, witchity, witchity, witch."

I didn't need to see it. I knew the masked face was peering out at me. It was there. And spring came that moment, unmistakably, musically, unexpectedly.

SWALLOWS

And gathering swallows twitter in the skies
—*Keats*

*I*T WAS LATE SUMMER. Two days before, the warm humid days had ended abruptly and through the early morning there was an autumnal crispness in the air. The sea, always beautiful, even when almost invisible in the fog, glittered freshly under cloudless skies, its deeper blue easing toward the sharp flat horizon and the lighter blue above. The brightness was almost painful. For once, my entire family was under one roof, gathering at the edge of autumn. David and his friend Becca, whom we had come to treat as a daughter, had arrived two weeks after Marge and I had settled into the house in Maine. He seemed as usual girded for a week without his writing and with the family; she seemed pleased and grateful and ready to fill the awkward holes in conversation and activity that David's unease and our ineptness in relation to it usually created. Rachel and Dale drove up at five in the morning,

159

three days later, from a hard summer's work in the theater at Cold Spring, bringing of course young Aaron, for whom we were waiting eagerly. They needed the rest. Until they all arrived, my greatest summer anxiety had been the size of my summer bird list, which had reached sixty-four; but with time running out and the available breeding species in the area largely counted—at least I thought so—I wasn't expecting to enlarge the list before we departed. In any case, this was a time to put aside merely personal pleasures and circle round once again the intimacies and tensions of a family—five terrific people with complex relations to us and to each other, making our lives richer and more difficult.

For me, late summer is somehow more disturbing than fall, when the inexorability of ending is clearly evident and when putting aside personal pleasures is daily routine. The end of August, usually deceptively warm and relaxed and abundant, comes also with shorter days, brief intimations of autumnal fruitfulness and decline, and yet another birthday. It is hard for me then not to think a lot about time, to feel its pressures, its subtle darkenings. I remember the first line of an adolescent sonnet I wrote before I had a right to: "They grieve, the keen-eyed, soon at summer's wane," and wonder despite the pretension and the mixtures of tone and the desperate attempt to sound pretty why it was that even back then August hurt so much.

I had for no reason I can account for learned early to be sensitive to subtle hints of change. As in February and early March I watch the blackbirds return, hear the cardinals start singing mating songs in the snow, watch the dull red of the house finches brighten a bit, so in August I watch the birds fall away from their breeding plumages, late season flowers begin to flourish, the fresh green of spring give way not only to the darker green of the mature leaf but to marks of decay that rapidly spread through the bushes and woods, where browns and reds begin to replace greens almost everywhere. And at the gathering in the house, my children seem older than I imagine myself to be, my grandson is becoming touchingly articulate in his early spring, my mirror reflects the appropriateness of his calling me Zaydee.

It is a gloriously melancholy time, every image pointing back to the lushness of the hot summer and forward to the austerity of winter. As I watch the still backwaters from the receding tide, the quiet mirroring of rocks and gulls and ducks in the gently refracted blue of the sky, the spotted sandpiper bobbing on rocks just recently underwater, Bonaparte's gulls with their heads still predominantly black looking very small and elegant against the herring and black-backed gulls, larger flocks of eider holding close inshore, and the sun everywhere, it is difficult not to feel the fragility of the moment. As the tide recedes, the sense of incompleteness and limits is most intense. I am happy to have son and daughter together with us again. I like and admire them both, but in the midst of all this and the peculiar pleasures of being able to give them holidays that they can't quite afford yet on their own, I enjoy very much rising alone early and keeping the dawn and the sea and the shorebirds for myself. Even when the children were small, I treasured the early morning hours and resented when they or Marge had reasons to be up with me.

At night I was feeling the melancholy in the darkness, and with the sun shining more brightly than it had for several days, I got up before six, as quietly as I could, not only to spare the family an early wakening but to protect the time. There was a sharp chill in the air. When I got downstairs and stared out toward the brilliant water, I gathered up a sweatshirt for some protection against a coldness sufficient to allow me to see my breath. There was some strange activity out front that turned out to be more birds than I had seen in a month of careful scanning. The bushes that join the house's yard with my neighbors' were filled entirely with birds. And clearly the birds were all swallows, not five or ten swallows, but hundreds. The power and telephone wires near the bushes were lined with birds, and my neighbor's roof was dotted with them. Their sheer movement was bewildering as they twittered, darted, replaced each other, spun up in clusters, settled back in the spots they had left after making large erratic circles. I had been thinking of trying just one last time to get an early morning hour of birds by cycling to Cape Porpoise and checking the water and the mudflats there in the unlikely event that at this late time, not fall yet and not quite summer, some bird I hadn't seen this year would turn up a little prematurely. But the action was in my backyard, unexpected and delightful and perhaps just a bit ominous. The swallows hadn't been there in the early weeks of my stay; they weren't going to be there again, even tomorrow.

Barn swallows, I thought, the most common swallows and ones that I had been seeing very frequently all summer. But it didn't take a very concentrated look to notice that only some of the birds had the characteristic long forked tail of the barn swallow and that many of them had white breasts, not the barn swallow's buff. Paul's injunction, which had become a maxim for us, was "check every bird." It's an injunction that's not as easy to carry out as it might seem, especially when there are hundreds of birds to count. But scanning intensely for differences could help: perhaps there were a few birds not barn swallows nor whatever the white-breasted ones were. So I walked quietly down the path in the brilliant, chilly sun, a little anxious that I would spook the birds.

These birds didn't spook. Their intensity was remarkable and gave me the feeling that I was witnessing a critical ritual moment in their lives, but as a result I had plenty of time to look and to measure the excitement I was feeling against the quiet of the house and against the probable lack of excitement that would follow upon its awakening if the family were to see me down here binoculars in hand staring into my neighbor's yard. While the scene would have caught—briefly—the attention of most non-birders, what I was excited about really required some birding experience. Discriminating different species of swallows is not everybody's idea of excitement or pleasure. And only someone who had already been paying attention would have felt how distinctly different these birds' behavior was from what they had been doing through most of the summer and how significant this was in our measure of time.

This clustering agitated behavior had to be a mark of seasonal change. The swallows' response to the recent radical shift in weather and in the texture of the air meant for them anticipation of southward migration, for me much the same—back to New Jersey and the conditions that drove me to Maine in the first place. These, I felt, would be relatively early migrants. After the tree swallows leave in September or early October, the skies would be empty of swallows again until the following May, and my pleasure in catching these birds just before their departure prepared me for that emptiness. I had no illusions about what the activity betokened and my exuberance at the sight was tempered by that knowledge.

I guess that most passersby, if they noticed the noisy activity themselves, would settle for the word "swallows." But of course, there are a lot of different kinds of swallows, and these, it turned out, were not as obvious as they first seemed. Standing ten yards from my house, I trained my binoculars on the power wires, shifting my position rapidly, sometimes to trace the flight of one of the birds, sometimes to see a different cluster, on the bushes, the trees, the power lines, the roofs. I was pleased to be able to see immediately that most of the birds I was watching were *not* barn swallows. Every detail of their appearance except the darting flight marked the difference: white breasts, broad, barely forked tails, with no touch of white on their edges, no buff on the face, brownish backs.

These are the kinds of distinctions that get my heart pumping faster but are unlikely to interest my family. Holding the distinctions in my head, perceiving the swallows with my glasses gave me another minute purchase on life. With mosquitoes working at my bare thighs and calves, I spent minutes on the path trying to make sure I knew what I was seeing. To distinguish the white-breasted bird from tree and bank swallows was a bit harder, but I was certain that the most abundant bird on the power line was the northern rough-winged swallow. Its white breast ends at the neck in a sort of dirty wash, varying from bird to bird, up to the throat and chin. Following the movements of any single swallow is very difficult, but there were so many birds to watch here, front view, back view, side view, darting or still, that I gradually became confident of the rough-winged identification.

Pleased as I was, these were not at all lifebirds for me: I had never seen a lot of rough-wings at a time, but during spring migration, as I check large flocks of barn and tree swallows, I am likely to find several of them, especially if they sit still for a few seconds. The book says that rough-wings tend to migrate singly or in "small flocks." I wouldn't have called what I was watching a "small" flock, but these certainly were rough-wings, and they certainly were behaving differently from any that I had seen before. They probably weren't migrating yet, but they were thinking about it.

In spite of what the mosquitoes were doing to my legs, I didn't want to quit on what was, for me, so rare a display. It wasn't time for a lifebird dance, but almost as pleasurable as seeing a lifebird is watching familiar birds do unfamiliar things. It was a summer bonus, an extra, given to me at the moment the arc of the summer had started curving downward and I had begun thinking of endings. Much as I hate mosquito bites, I accepted them in exchange for this revelation in my backyard.

Unfortunately, time moves as rapidly as the swallows, and if I wanted to get in some morning exercise before the house awoke, I had to start doing it immediately. Paul's injunction thrust itself forward, however, and having identified barn and rough-wing swallows, I needed to see if there were any others: in particular, to check again for tree swallows and bank swallows. Although nothing I saw corresponded to these, there was something rather unfamiliar about a few of the birds that I couldn't quite figure out. The barn swallow is distinctive, of course, and its cinnamon and buff coloring and slate blue-gray back make it stand out among many of the American swallows. Whenever my eye registered those colors, I told myself barn swallows. Except that some of those buff-bellied birds were not showing the lengthy and diagnostic tail.

In the midst of these tense internal negotiations with reality, I had slipped entirely out of the family mode. My mind is rarely so concentrated as when I am on the edge of naming a bird. I was so intent that I didn't even think out of the corner of my mind what I am aware of in the writing, how much I hoped nobody in the house would perceive or call me at this moment. Not even Aaron would have been welcome. Although I prefer most of the time to go birding with a companion, I wouldn't ever want to give up the moments in the field alone.

If birding in solitude loses the possibility of intense companionship when things go right and the relief from uncertainty that comes with another's informed opinion, it has the virtue, among other things, of putting me entirely in charge of my birding fate. The satisfaction of working it out for oneself, of knowing what to look for and how to look for it, of wrestling it through so that the name undoubtedly fits, of being privy to something that feels important and that the rest of the world is too preoccupied to notice is an almost unique feeling in my experience. The alternative one of sharing has its own power: I love to have real birders with me in the woods or even in situations like this, in part because I know that when on the edge of such moments they will understand what is at stake. And no doubt if I had another birder with me, that

swallow on the railing would have declared itself unequivo-
cally by now. But I was working it through without any help
and feeling so good about it that I didn't even know at the
moment that I was feeling good.

Alone, I had to resist the temptation to name the bird I had
just guessed was there, declare myself satisfied, and move on
to other things. It was still more than just possible that I was
deceiving myself because as I concentrated on finding once
again those few anomalous birds I thought I had seen, they
were gone. Barn swallows and rough-wings were everywhere
and totally filled the wires and bushes. I knew I couldn't claim
the elusive swallow and was beginning to think about rejecting once more my instinctive sense of things, and chalking
this one up to illusion and desire. I could get on my bike for a
quick ride to the mudflats and another set of birds and bird
problems designed to resist the autumn.

But among the dozens of rough-wings and several barn
swallows, there appeared finally almost magically again a bird,
its back to me, sitting on the wire, looking different. I was
ready for it this time and for the distinctive cinnamon rump
showing on what otherwise might have seemed a barn
swallow's back—a rump that was diagnostic of the cliff swallow. This one didn't get away, and I kept my glasses focused
on it to catch it when it moved, waiting to see if its tail would
betray in yet another way its difference from the barn swallow.
Another flew in to join it, species comrade in a world of other
sorts of swallows, and its tail showed almost flat. When they
both moved, there could be no doubt. They were different
and they had a name by which I could know them.

Declining eyesight, declining skills, declining memory had
not prevented me from knowing what nobody else around me
knew. There were three kinds of swallows making this unusual
racket and turbulence on a late summer morning—the barn,
the rough-winged, and now, I knew, the cliff. Cliff swallows
aren't rare, but I see them only occasionally, some years if I'm

unlucky, I don't see them at all. It wasn't a lifebird, but it was a yearbird, and I was ridiculously vain about being so confident about a bird so unfamiliar to me.

The summer continued to yield its fruits. It was a good day. Later, walking on the beach, David and I spotted a loon in non-breeding plumage, and across the road, on the marsh, a willet with zebra-striped wings. He indulged my enthusiasm, professed enough interest in the loon to borrow my binoculars. We talked more comfortably in the softening air than I had expected, although we had to squint away from the still brilliant sun. The summer was ending with family confidences and it seemed almost as rich as the morning, when three kinds of swallows filled the bushes, reminding me in my momentary and necessary solitude, of the life and the entanglements that are sustained beyond summer.

wood duck

WOODCOCK

At evening, casual flocks of pigeons make
ambiguous undulations as they sink,
downward to darkness on extended wings.
—Wallace Stevens

WHAT BIRD could provide a fitting conclusion to these open-ended meditations? Perhaps I will have to run through each of the 399 American species I have more or less confidently identified: the cedar waxwing I first saw eating red berries on a bush near the shore on my first visit to Ogunquit, Maine; the romantic sounding wandering tatler looking grayly undistinguished on a beach just south of Los Angeles; the acorn woodpeckers hammering away at the facade over the entrance to the Stanford University library; the osprey soaring over a cliff near Highway 1 that almost killed me as I tried to identify it and maneuver the curves on the road to Mendocino; the scarlet tanager illuminating the woods behind Livingston College, Rutgers; the flicker sitting on a lawn in an industrial park just four blocks from my home; the surfbird, suddenly visible on enormous rocks after the violence of the Oregon surf had made me think no living thing could withstand that force.

These birds and the hundreds of others that get check marks in my AOU bird list make images of beginnings, not endings. They open up for me in their vividness large sequences and major entanglements of my life that might otherwise have been lost, as much of my life—and, I suspect, most other lives—has been lost, in irretrievable memories. The images make narratives and meaning out of complications and confusions and multiplicities, all of which they evoke, yet all of which they tend to control. My family was in the car when the osprey flew over, crooked-winged, powerful, graceful, and in my excitement I almost drove off the cliff: George, keep your eyes on the road. I was alone and surprised by the flicker as I drove to work in the morning with my mind on other things and discovered that such a remarkable creature, with its striking woodpecker shape, red patch on its neck, gray crown, dark cream face, black necklace, yellow-white spotted breast, and woody woodpecker laugh could live so cozily in the suburbs. I was alone when I saw the surfbird, on an Oregon trip that I was prolonging for just such moments while Marge was tending to her sick mother. There is a moment, a place, a relationship in each of these birds. Reflection makes them multiple and each bird gathers around its distinctive and humanly independent stance, flight, colors and sound all the complexities and uncertainties that, in my sighting of it in the field, seem momentarily dispelled. Each of them, however, produces a moment of serenity, of deep satisfaction, transitory as the flight of a swallow through a barn, but lastingly illuminating and expansive.

It's comforting to know that I will never see all the species in the world (which number, I think, close to nine thousand). I will not even see all the American species. There is always a new bird to find. Despite the satisfactions of clarity and meaning that birds sometimes bring with them, the lack of an ending is central to the experience of birding. And it's not simply expectation of another lifebird. No matter how many times I see a yellowthroat in April, I go out in the next April with similar enthusiasm to see it or its inheritors again.

But even those selected 399 images, multiplied in most cases by uncounted later sightings, which entail revisions of my sense of their identity, constitute the smallest and perhaps the least characteristic fragment if also the most immediately satisfying of my birding experiences. They focus meaning and identity. Most birds remain for me unnamed or ambiguous, and they escape back into their worlds without ever confirming my guesses, or revealing their identities at all. In the East, there is a genus of flycatchers called empidonax that includes five distinct species. I use the word "distinct" without reference to what can in fact be perceived, because the five species are virtually indistinguishable, even for experts, except by their calls. If they choose to remain silent—which seems to happen for me most of the time—I can register them only as "empidonax," but not as "alder," "Acadian," "least," "yellow-bellied," or "willow." Paul's maxim that not every bird was meant to be identified is in fact a saving maxim, for even in areas where I feel at home and never hear an unfamiliar voice, where the songs have become second nature to me, most of what I see and hear remains at the very least ambiguous. I've tested myself a few times when out walking: identify every bird sound you hear, I have urged myself, and within seconds I am in despair. The sounds are all familiar and many of them require no reflection. But there are hundreds of "chips" and squeaks, familiar sounds that I can't for the moment classify, variations that seem in the instant possible for several different species. The house finch, as common a bird as there is in my area, turns up in more places than I can quickly see. Something flies by rapidly and I get only a sense of movement. Squabbling chickadees make unchickadee-like sounds. Mourning doves seem for a moment like kestrels. Sometimes I pause to work out an immediate puzzle and even if I manage, I lose several other birds that won't quite be characteristic or entirely visible. Most of the time I continue about my business, whatever it happens to be, and leave the bird's identity to itself. Sometimes, songs with which I am familiar turn out not to be familiar, with quite shaking implications. I have only recently, for example, discovered that the laughing call of the flicker is virtually identical with the call of the pileated woodpecker, one of the most striking birds in America, and one that through bad fortune and only moderate birding skills I see infrequently. I now realize that when in the woods I hear the "kik-kik-kik" laugh of the flicker and I don't even bother to look up because I am so confident of the bird and have other more difficult species to locate, I might well be missing a pileated, laughing down at me. Of course, the flicker is much more common and much more easy to find. But my confidence in the identification by sound of so familiar a bird as the flicker is shaken, and while the books indicate that the "kik-kik-kik" of the pileated is higher and louder, I couldn't tell the call of the pileated I heard two months ago from the hundreds of flickers I have heard through two decades of springs.

And there are times when parts of the titmouse call sound like a chickadee, when robins sound like vireos, when mockingbirds sound like virtually any bird, when starlings, with their often grotesque squeaks and rattles, can sound like far prettier birds, when finch calls seem to overlap, when parts of a towhee's call sound like a woodthrush, when the voices of the thrushes confuse me, when the Babel of birdsound is so rich that it's impossible to extricate and isolate all of the implicit strands of life. There is more bird life even in my suburban neighborhood than I can put in order. As I walk through that neighborhood, with all its familiar voices, I realize that any sense of order to which I might cling is based almost entirely on each bird's most characteristic call. Most of the time I fool myself into not knowing that I am in fact rejecting the complications and the static of the birds' multiplicities. Even the most obvious birds have individual qualities and most birds have a whole range of calls and alarm notes, adjusted to different functions, like mating or defending territory.

Lifebirds, then, in the moments when they reveal themselves to me, are truly rarities. Through most of my birding life I move as thoroughly uncomprehending, as uneasily bent on finding out, as when I am at other work and in other relationships. The difference in birding, perhaps, is that spending the time searching is always a kind of pleasure, even when it exposes me to bitter cold or murderous insects. Finally, it will occasionally and usually unexpectedly provide me with rare moments of revelation, when the abundance, complexity, difficulty, multiplicity of Darwin's tangled bank—which is beautiful in its own difficult way—are resolved into a clear voice, a clear image, a name. Within the disorder and Babel there was always lurking this singular bird, which I now can name before it slips back into the brush or the higher branches of inaccessible trees. When a young woman walking through my neighborhood saw me looking intently at a tree from which a bird was making the insistent call that Peterson translates as "peter, peter, peter," she paused curiously. "I've been hearing that bird for a while. Do you know what it is?" With a flush of absurd but undeniable pride, I told her: "It's a tufted titmouse." And I showed her the picture in the field guide I was carrying. Nothing difficult in that identification but I know that in a very small way I transformed the place for her, made her understand what it was that had always been sharing the neighborhood with her. The naming and the picture made a difference.

In the end, the birds, of course, resolve nothing: they simply offer moments like that, evidence of other and beautiful forms of life. Knowing that the life exists is sufficient pleasure. To be privileged to know that it exists and to understand some minute portion of it is part of what makes me a birder. Despite the birds' ultimate refusal to accept my identifications of them, to be subject to the anthropomorphizing and sentimentalizing fantasies to which I—and most birders—are prone, to wear the name tags that would make every sighting a certainty, they somehow learn to say "peter, peter, peter" if they are titmice, and an "emphatic teach'er, TEACH'ER, TEACH'ER" if they are ovenbirds, and thus help me through difficulties. Our relations are of course thoroughly compromised by my requirement that they talk like me even though I know they don't. We agree to accept the terms of our necessities but are under no illusions about how much we really understand each other.

I know that they are there and complicated and beautiful and I devise whatever strategies are necessary to find and name them. I take the ambiguities and uncertainties as thoroughly as I take the moments of revelation. Those ambiguities and uncertainties may in time suddenly crystallize into revelation, but the tensions of doubt and irresolution, disallowing the comforts of clear identification, point toward a richness and fertility that naming could only constrict. Nature, like everything else, escapes our language, but through it we build alternative places to evoke and do honor to what we can't ultimately name.

I end with two twilights. One, a last gesture to day, the other, a descent into night: two birds, one assimilating itself to the desires of the humans who seemed to evoke it, the other insisting on its own distinctly non-human life and posterity.

The first was a twilight extraordinarily serene and satisfying. It was after a bird-filled day at the Brigantine, that virtual Disneyland of birding across from Atlantic City, where one can almost always count on abundance. Paul and I would have been exhausted after the long day as we became aware that twilight was coming on, but we were so exhilarated by the day's discoveries that we were not quite ready to quit. As the darkness settled in over the still waters, both of us were feeling very good, very pleased with ourselves, deeply satisfied. And as we drove the last yards of the sanctuary on the dirt road that surrounds the bird-rich ponds, Paul suggested that we use the last remaining light at the exit. It was getting a little hard to see, but there was a pearly light reflecting off the quiet water, and we got out of the car one last time to scan the ponds on both sides of the road. Almost with surprise because it had been such a bird-rich day, Paul noted as we scanned, "We never did see a wood duck today."

It was like a witch's spell: quietly, without even rippling the water, a mature male wood duck glided before us, its bold and eccentric markings clearly recognizable even in the dimming light. The sudden manifestation was so serendipitous and so quietly, calmingly mysterious, that while both of us have seen many wood ducks in our birding lives, we both know exactly what we mean when one of us says, "Remember the wood duck at the Brigantine?" Dark as it was growing, it remains the most beautiful and satisfying sighting of the wood duck I have ever had, and there were no doubts: "The bizarre face pattern, swept-back crest, and rainbow iridescence are unique."

The second twilight followed upon a yet more exciting birding day. It was the second full day of our trip to Point Pelee, which was filled with birds and with others who were thriving on them. Earlier, as I stood with Paul on the edge of the road catching some movement in the trees, I focused my glasses and found a lovely Canada warbler, black necklace across brilliant yellow throat and belly, and called, "Paul, there's a Canada." When I looked up to see if Paul had found it, I discovered that he was nowhere near me but I was surrounded with ten or a dozen strangers, glasses to their eyes, "Where? where is it?" It was that kind of day, and I wasn't even disturbed by the presence of all those others seeking my birds. But I was not feeling the peace of the twilight in the Brigantine: an almost manic energy had kept me going without pause from five in the morning. The instant birding community at the Point, where hundreds of enthusiasts swapped information with each other at the flash of the binoculars, led us to understand that just at dusk woodcock would be performing their ritual mating dance and song in an area of hilly dunes not far from where we were birding. I had seen woodcock before, but I had never seen or heard the ritual dance. Paul, of course, was eager to wait it out. To my surprise, Michael, who was more interested in us than in the birds, although he was interested in them too, seemed eager to watch the promised display.

It was getting chilly as the sun's rays angled acutely across. We were all exhausted but exhilarated too in our fashion, and we began our vigil wishing we had some slightly heavier clothes. There were at least a half dozen others there, waiting for the woodcock, wondering exactly where he would turn up. I remember hearing, to my right, the dry buzzing of a warbler I always like to see, and, just a bit anxiously, I turned away to locate it: the worm-eating warbler, a bird we hadn't seen yet that day, was clearly in a grove just off the dunes. It was a relatively easy identification and my fear that I would have missed something in this detour turned out to be unwarranted. Nothing had happened in the woodcock alert. There were speculations about where he would turn up and we began moving off in the direction suggested by a birder who seemed the most knowledgeable in the group.

I was by then trembling with cold, but the discomfort was minor in comparison to the expectation. My greatest concern was that it was getting too dark to see any birds at all. My eyes are bad enough in the daylight, but in the dim light of evening they are almost useless. None of us, however, gave the slightest thought to giving up and leaving.

"This way," the expert sharply whispered. "This way." It was a little hard to see now but I stumbled with the rest of them to a hilly area in time to hear someone at the site urgently whisper: "Listen, it's up." I listened and there was an odd twittering that ascended until it seemed almost beyond earshot, and then came an audible and rapid descent in a new and remarkable voice. I thought I saw the bird silhouetted against the pale, darkening sky. But then began another ritual of display in the incipient darkness. "At dusk in spring," says Peterson, "the female utters a nasal *beezp*"—which in fact was what had attracted the expert to the spot in the first place. "Aerial 'song,' a chippering trill (made by wings) as bird ascends, changing to a burbling warble on descent."

I heard the *beezp*, the trill, and the burbling warble, and all the sounds of woodcock intimacy. But when the burbling warble stopped I couldn't be sure that I had seen the bird land. I couldn't be sure that I had seen the bird at all. The twilight was utterly quiet except for the agitated whispers of the birders and the sound of the almost lunatic woodcock making those mad and wonderful ascents and descents.

I knew the woodcock was there, and I knew its ritual was an affirmation of its sexual prowess to some other beezping woodcock below, which didn't need the light to know what it wanted. I was thrilled by the sound and by the "sighting," but as I stared intently into what had suddenly become a virtual darkness, I could see at best only the last outlines of a silhouette fade into uniformity with its background. While the sound recurred now mysteriously, tracing an invisible flight, an arc that curved finally back to earth, I felt neither chilled nor earthbound. Yet I do not know what the flight or the bird looked like and to this day I am not sure that I actually saw the bird or that I was doing anything but translating the texts I knew describing the experience into the experience itself.

Again, the bird didn't care: nature was pricking him in his "corages," and the elaborate sexual display was not for me but for other birds. Warm with a sense of knowledge and contact with the friends who were with me and a world I would never really understand, I was witness to a ritual performed by a bird that remained unknown and finally disappeared into the darkness.

About the Author

George Levine is Kenneth Burke Professor of English at Rutgers University, and author of many books about Victorian literature and culture, including *Darwin and the Novelists*. He is married to the artist Marge Levine, father of stage manager Rachel Levine and writer David Levine, and grandfather of Aaron Michael Thompson.